2020
ASTROLOGY
ORACLE CARD PLANNER

A FUN, CREATIVE PLANNER & WORKBOOK TO MAKE THE MOST OF YOUR ASTROLOGICAL ENERGY

BY HEATHER ARIELLE
ARTWORK BY THOM CUMMINS

LUMINOUS MOON PRESS
BOULDER, COLORADO

A COMPANION TO

THE FUNDAMENTALS OF
ASTROLOGY: A 52-CARD
DECK AND GUIDEBOOK

Text copyright © 2013-2020 Heather Hill All Rights Reserved
www.HouseOfAstrology.com

Artwork copyright © 1980 Thom Cummins

Published by Luminous Moon Press
3980 Broadway St, Ste 103-115
Boulder, Colorado 80304
www.LuminousMoon.com
First published in 2020

ISBN: 978-0-9968600-8-6
Printed in the USA

How To Make the Most of Your Astrological Energy in 2020

Use this Astrology Oracle Card Planner to strengthen your intuition and to explore personal, practical, and powerful ways astrology can improve your daily life.

To do the inspirational readings and spreads outlined in the Planner, you will need a tarot or oracle deck. Although not essential, in order to have the most in-depth experience, it is recommended that the Planner be used in conjunction with Heather Arielle's The Fundamentals of Astrology: A 52 Card Deck and Guidebook. The set is available from Amazon and many Body/Mind/Spirit bookshops and stores.

It is also recommended that you have a copy of your Natal Chart. If you don't have one, there are many online services that will prepare a chart for you, or order a PDF Natal Chart from Heather Arielle for $25 at **AriellesAstrology.com**.

WHAT IS ASTROLOGY?

Astrology is the study of the positions of the planets, stars, and other celestial bodies at the exact moment and location of your birth and how these positions influence your life.

WHAT IS A NATAL CHART?

A Natal Chart is a snapshot of the cosmos the moment you are born. This is a fixed chart. It does not change at any point in your life. A Natal Chart is what an astrologer refers to/works off of whenever you receive an astrological reading. In order to create your Natal Chart, the location and exact time of your birth are required.

ASTROLOGY IS FULL OF NUANCE AND DUALITY

No Zodiac Sign is good or bad, helpful or hurtful, lucky or unlucky. Each sign has its strengths, as well as its temptations. I have created an astrology oracle deck to capture the nuance and duality inherent in each Zodiac Sign, Planet, and House.

When you are in balance with your energy, you will more easily manifest your talents and gifts; but when you are out of balance, you are more likely to give in to temptations and self-sabotaging behavior.

By incorporating this deck into your daily life, you will gain awareness of your full astrological potential. Areas that are out of balance will be illuminated. And then the choice is yours, "Do I want to be *in* or *out* of balance with my energy?" Because you have free will, it is up to you to decide.

WHAT ARE CUSPS AND ANGLES?

The first degree of an astrological House is also known as its Cusp. The four Angles (Ascendant, Imum Coeli, Descendant, and Medium Coeli) are on the Cusps of your First House, Fourth House, Seventh House, and Tenth House respectively. They are sensitive triggers for the issues of their houses.

Read more in Heather Arielle's Guidebook for The Fundamentals of Astrology.

ASTROLOGY ACTIVITIES INCLUDED IN THE PLANNER

Each time the Sun, Mercury, Venus, and Mars enter new Zodiac Signs, you will have the opportunity to explore how the new energy will affect you in personal, practical, and profoundly powerful ways. And, of course, if your Natal Planet is in that Sign, then these gifts are open to you all year around.

Each astrology activity offers an advanced option for those of you desiring an even deeper knowledge of your astrological potential. For the purpose of these activities, when a Sign covers two Houses in your chart, select the House that has the Cusp in that Sign to complete the activity.

Sample of a Traditional Natal Chart

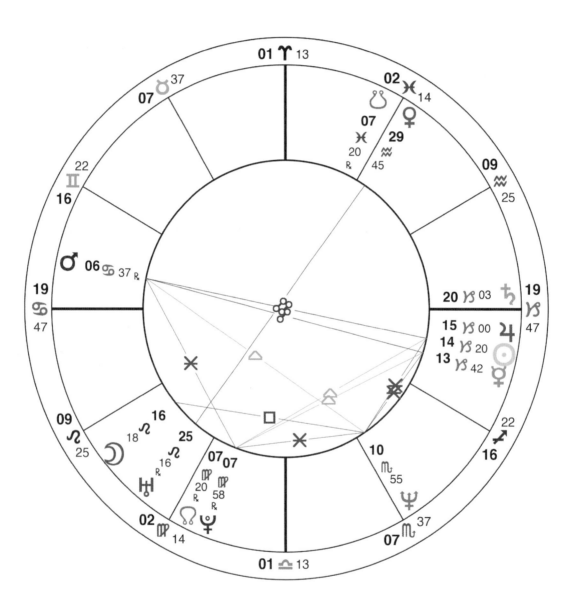

Three Main Elements of a Natal Chart: Houses, Planets, and Signs

HOUSES

There are 12 boxes or squares on a traditional Natal Chart. Each box corresponds to an area of experience known in astrological terms as a House. So each chart is made up of 12 Houses.

1st House: Self-identity
2nd House: Earned income
3rd House: Siblings, early education, and current neighborhood
4th House: Home, family, ancestors
5th House: Children, creativity, romance
6th House: Work, health, and daily routine
7th House: One-on-one partnerships (personal and professional)
8th House: Death, taxes, inheritances, joint resources
9th House: Higher education, long distance travel, publicity
10th House: Public status, professional calling, parents, marriage
11th House: Friends, hopes and dreams, organizations
12th House: Secret/hidden knowledge, matters of spirituality, and consciousness

PLANETS

You Are More Than Just Your Sun Sign

It's important to remember that you are so much more than just your Sun sign (Gemini, Aquarius, Scorpio, etc.). Because astrology is refined and complicated, it has been overly simplified and boiled down over the years to focus only on zodiac Sun signs.

Although the Sun is very important in a Natal Chart, it is one of only **five personal planets**: Sun, Moon, Mercury, Venus, and Mars. (Note that in astrology, the Sun, Moon, and Chiron are referred to as planets, even though the Sun is a star, the Moon is an astronomical body that orbits the Earth, and Chiron is a comet.) They exert great power in your Natal Chart, and their power is what is important to understand.

Personal Planets (You can read more about these in the Guidebook for The Fundamentals of Astrology on pages 107–127.)

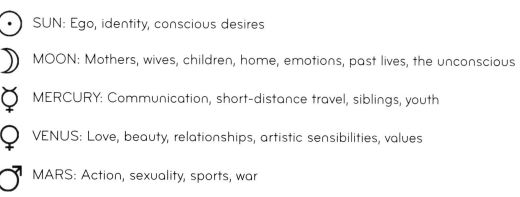

SUN: Ego, identity, conscious desires

MOON: Mothers, wives, children, home, emotions, past lives, the unconscious

MERCURY: Communication, short-distance travel, siblings, youth

VENUS: Love, beauty, relationships, artistic sensibilities, values

MARS: Action, sexuality, sports, war

Outer Planets

The **five outer planets** are Jupiter, Saturn, Uranus, Neptune, and Pluto. For our purposes, I also include a card for Chiron in the 52-card deck. (You can read more about the outer planets and Chiron in the Guidebook for The Fundamentals of Astrology on pages 128-156.)

♃ JUPITER: Expansive, optimistic, abundant

♄ SATURN: Restrictive, adult, karmic

♅ URANUS: Electrifying, disruptive, awakening

♆ NEPTUNE: Spiritual, transcendent, poetic

♇ PLUTO: Transformative, powerful, karmic

⚷ CHIRON: Healing, sensitive, karmic

ZODIAC SIGNS

The Western Zodiac is a seasonal zodiac and begins with the first day of spring, 0 degrees Aries. All together there are 12 Zodiac Signs. When you look up your horoscope, you are looking up your Zodiac Sun Sign.

♈ ARIES: Pioneering and visionary

♉ TAURUS: Enduring and stable

♊ GEMINI: Playful and curious

♋ CANCER: Nurturing and protective

♌ LEO: Outgoing and dramatic

♍ VIRGO: Desiring to be of service

♎ LIBRA: Desiring of equality and justice

♏ SCORPIO: Passionate and transformative

♐ SAGITTARIUS: Desiring freedom and expansion

♑ CAPRICORN: Manifesting in tangible ways

♒ AQUARIUS: Unique, rebellious, and humanitarian

♓ PISCES: Sensitive, poetic, and creative

Inspirational Spreads Included in the Astrology Oracle Card Planner

MONTHLY INSPIRATIONAL READING

Each month when the Sun changes zodiac signs, perform your monthly inspirational reading. Ask your guides to inspire and prepare you for the month. Choose a card. Reflect on your inspirational message, and be sure to record it in the planner. This card will represent an overall theme to incorporate into your life while the Sun is in that zodiac sign.

WEEKLY INSPIRATIONAL READING

Each week, do a simple one-card inspirational reading to inspire and prepare you for the week. Be sure to record your message.

NEW MOON SPREAD

Each month, there is a New Moon; the time between a New and Full Moon is a powerful two-week window when whatever you start or develop will grow and blossom. It's especially important to be present with your energy during this time. I've developed a unique and comprehensive spread that highlights the most beneficial astrological aspects to incorporate during these important periods. Perform the New Moon Spread at the start of every New Moon. For more detailed instructions, watch my YouTube video, "New Moon Astrology Oracle Card Spread by Heather Arielle."

Link: https://youtu.be/kogl5q7-hH4

MERCURY, VENUS, AND MARS RETROGRADES

Remember my motto during retrogrades: If You Can RE-It, You Can Do It!

Every **Mercury Retrograde** (there are three in 2020: February 16-March 10, June 18-July 12, and October 13-November 3), perform the Mercury Retrograde Spread. Retrogrades are deeply personal and reflective times, and this spread will help you to recalibrate and rejuvenate during these energies.

Venus Retrograde: Perform the Venus Retrograde spread during the one Venus retrograde that takes place in 2020 (May 13-June25). This spread will help you to review, reevaluate, and reignite your relationships.

Mars Retrograde: Perform the Mars Retrograde spread during the one Mars retrograde that takes place in 2020 (September 9-November 13). This spread will highlight the Mars areas (health, temperament, and ability to take action) that are in most need of revitalization.

ENJOY AND EMBRACE TRANSFORMATION!

May you experience your highest levels of joy, creativity, consciousness, bliss, and abundance!

–Heather Arielle

Want to go more in-depth? Have questions about your chart or the messages of your spreads? I am here to help! Call 917-546-6797 for a reading or book online at AriellesAstrology.com.

2020 Moon Phase Timings

FULL MOON			NEW MOON		
Jan 10 Penumbral Lunar Eclipse	2:21 PM	20 Can 00'	Jan 24	4:42 PM	4 Aqu 22'
Feb 9	2:33 AM	20 Leo 00'	Feb 23	10:32 AM	4 Pis 29'
Mar 9	1:48 PM	19 Vir 37'	Mar 24	5:28 AM	4 Ari 12'
Apr 7	10:35 PM	18 Lib 44'	Apr 22	10:26 PM	3 Tau 24'
May 7	6:45 AM	17 Sco 20'	May 22	1:39 PM	2 Gem 05'
Jun 5 Penumbral LUNAR Eclipse	3:12 PM	15 Sag 34'	Jun 21 Annular SOLAR Eclipse	2:41 AM	0 Can 21'
Jul 5 Penumbral LUNAR Eclipse	12:44 AM	13 Cap 38'	Jul 20	1:33 PM	28 Can 27'
Aug 3	11:59 AM	11 Aqu 46'	Aug 18	10:42 PM	26 Leo 35'
Sep 2	1:22 AM	10 Pis 12'	Sep 17	7:00 AM	25 Vir 01'
Oct 1	5:05 PM	9 Ari 08'	Oct 16	3:31 PM	23 Lib 53'
Oct 31	10:49 AM	8 Tau 38'	Nov 15	12:07 AM	23 Sco 18'
Nov 30 Penumbral LUNAR Eclipse	4:30 AM	8 Gem 38'	Dec 14 Total SOLAR Eclipse	11:16 AM	23 Sag 08'
Dec 29	10:28 PM	8 Can 53'			

- All times are local times for US Eastern Time
- Time is adjusted for daylight savings time when applicable. Please adjust for your state/country.
- Dates are based on the Gregorian calendar.

2020 Special Astrological Events

DATE	TIME (ET)	EVENT	POSITION
Jan 3	4:37 AM	Mars enters Sagittarius	Mar 0 Sag 00'
Jan 10	2:21 PM	Full Moon Penumbral Lunar Eclipse in Cancer	20 Can 00'
Jan 13	1:39 PM	Venus enters Pisces	Ven 0 Pis 00'
Jan 16	1:31 PM	Mercury enters Aquarius	Mer 0 Aqu 00'
Jan 20	9:55 AM	Sun enters Aquarius	Sun 0 Aqu 00'
Jan 24	4:42 PM	New Moon in Aquarius	4 Aqu 22'
Feb 3	6:37 AM	Mercury enters Pisces	Mer 0 Pis 00'
Feb 7	3:02 PM	Venus enters Aries	Ven 0 Ari 00'
Feb 9	2:33 AM	Full Moon in Leo	20 Leo 00'
Feb 16	6:33 AM	Mars enters Capricorn	Mars 0 Cap 00'
Feb 16	7:54 PM	Mercury Retrograde	Mer 12 Pis 53'Rx
Feb 18	11:57 PM	Sun enters Pisces	Sun 0 Pis 00'
Feb 23	10:32 AM	New Moon in Pisces	4 Pis 29'
Mar 4	6:07 AM	Mercury Retrograde enters Aquarius	Mer Aqu Rx
Mar 4	10:07 PM	Venus enters Taurus	Ven 0 Tau 00'
Mar 9	1:48 PM	Full Moon in Virgo	19 Vir 37'
Mar 9	11:49 PM	Mercury Direct	Mer 28 Aqu 13'D
Mar 16	3:42 AM	Mercury enters Pisces	Mer 0 Pis 00'
Mar 19	11:49 PM	Sun enters Aries	Sun 0 Ari 00'
Mar 24	5:28 AM	New Moon in Aries	4 Ari 12'
Mar 30	3:43 PM	Mars enters Aquarius	Mars 0 Aqu 00'
Apr 3	1:10 PM	Venus enters Gemini	Ven 0 Gem 00'
Apr 7	10:35 PM	Full Moon in Libra	18 Lib 44'
Apr 11	12:48 AM	Mercury enters Aries	Mer 0 Aries 00'
Apr 19	10:45 AM	Sun enters Taurus	Sun 0 Tau 00'
Apr 22	10:26 PM	New Moon in Taurus	3 Tau 24'
Apr 27	3:53 PM	Mercury enters Taurus	Mer 0 Tau 00'
May 7	6:45 AM	Full Moon in Scorpio	17 Sco 20'
May 11	5:58 PM	Mercury enters Gemini	Mer 0 Gem 00'
May 13	12:17 AM	Mars enters Pisces	Mars 0 Pis 00'
May 13	2:45 AM	Venus Retrograde	Ven 21 Gem 50'Rx
May 20	9:49 AM	Sun enters Gemini	Sun 0 Gem 00'
May 22	1:39 PM	New Moon in Gemini	2 Gem 05'
May 28	2:09 PM	Mercury enters Cancer	Mer 0 Can 00'
Jun 5	3:12 PM	Full Moon Penumbral LUNAR Eclipse in Sagittarius	15 Sag 34'
Jun 18	12:59 AM	Mercury Retrograde	Mer 14 Can 46'Rx
Jun 20	5:44 PM	Sun enters Cancer	Sun 0 Can 00'
Jun 21	2:41 AM	New Moon Annual SOLAR Eclipse in Cancer	0 Can 21'
Jun 25	2:48 AM	Venus Direct	Ven 5 Gem 20'D
Jun 27	9:45 PM	Mars enters Aries	Mar 0 Ari 00'
Jul 5	12:44 AM	Full Moon Penumbral LUNAR Eclipse	13 Cap 38'

Jul 12	4:26 AM	Mercury Direct	Mer 5 Can 30'D
Jul 20	1:33 PM	New Moon in Cancer	28 Can 27'
Jul 22	4:37 AM	Sun enters Leo	Sun 0 Leo 00'
Aug 3	11:59 AM	Full Moon in Aquarius	11 Aqu 46'
Aug 4	11:32 PM	Mercury enters Leo	Mer 0 Leo 00'
Aug 7	11:21 AM	Venus enters Cancer	Ven 0 Can 00'
Aug 18	10:42 PM	New Moon in Leo	26 Leo 35'
Aug 19	9:35 PM	Mercury enters Virgo	Mer 0 Vir 00'
Aug 22	11:45 AM	Sun enters Virgo	Sun 0 Vir 00'
Sep 2	1:22 AM	Full Moon	10 Pis 12'
Sep 5	3:46 PM	Mercury enters Libra	Mer 0 Lib 00'
Sep 6	3:21 AM	Venus enters Leo	Ven 0 Leo 00'
Sep 9	6:22 PM	Mars Retrograde	Mar 28 Ari 09'Rx
Sep 17	7:00 AM	New Moon in Virgo	25 Vir 01'
Sep 22	9:30 AM	Sun enters Libra	Sun 0 Lib 00'
Sep 27	3:40 AM	Mercury enters Scorpio	Mer 0 Sco 00'
Oct 1	5:05 PM	Full Moon in Aries	9 Ari 08'
Oct 2	4:48 PM	Venus enters Virgo	Ven 0 Vir 00'
Oct 13	9:05 PM	Mercury Retrograde	Mer 11 Sco 40'Rx
Oct 16	3:31 PM	New Moon in Libra	23 Lib 53'
Oct 22	6:59 PM	Sun enters Scorpio	Sun 0 Sco 00'
Oct 27	9:33 PM	Mercury Retrograde enters Libra	Mer Rx Lib
Oct 27	9:41 PM	Venus enters Libra	Ven 0 Lib 00'
Oct 31	10:49 AM	Full Moon in Taurus	8 Tau 38'
Nov 3	12:49 PM	Mercury Direct in Libra	Mer 25 Lib 54'D
Nov 10	4:55 PM	Mercury enters Scorpio	Mer 0 Sco 00'
Nov 13	7:35 PM	Mars Direct in Aries	Mars 15 Ari 14'D
Nov 15	12:07 AM	New Moon in Scorpio	23 Sco 18'
Nov 21	8:22 AM	Venus enters Scorpio	Ven 0 Sco 00'
Nov 21	3:40 PM	Sun enters Sagittarius	Sun 0 Sag 00'
Nov 30	4:30 AM	Full Moon Penumbral LUNAR Eclipse in Gemini	8 Gem 38'
Dec 1	2:51 PM	Mercury enters Sagittarius	Mer 0 Sag 00'
Dec 14	11:16 AM	New Moon Total SOLAR Eclipse in Sagittarius	23 Sag 08'
Dec 15	11:21 AM	Venus enters Sagittarius	Ven 0 Sag 00'
Dec 20	6:07 PM	Mercury enters Capricorn	Mer 0 Cap 00'
Dec 21	5:02 AM	Sun enters Capricorn	Sun 0 Cap 00'
Dec 29	10:28 PM	Full Moon in Cancer	8 Can 53'

- All times are local times for US Eastern Time
- Time is adjusted for daylight savings time when applicable. Please adjust for your state/country.
- Dates are based on the Gregorian calendar.

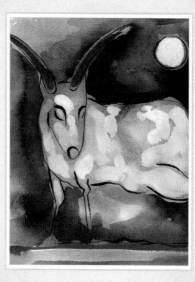

Capricorn
Climb Every Mountain

It's time to be the mountain goat and begin your ascent.

Humble Pie

Your ego is strong enough to survive a healthy dose of constructive criticism.

On December 21, 2019 the Sun moves into Capricorn, the tenth Sign of the Zodiac, and remains there until January 20. The expansive and optimistic energy of Sagittarius is transformed into the sober, practical, and restrictive energy of Capricorn. Ruled by Saturn, Capricorn is an earthy, sensible Sign, imparting its natives with all the tools they need to manifest in the real world.

Capricorn

Saturn

Planet: Saturn
House: Tenth
Element: Earth
Modality: Cardinal

IN BALANCE: In balance, Capricorns are wonderful self-starters. They are revered as the sages and elders of their community.

OUT OF BALANCE: Out of balance, they can begin to view their Capricorn talent for methodical self-discipline as more of a burden than a gift.

Sun in Capricorn

DECEMBER 21, 2019

Sun
Shine Your Light Brightly
Celebrate this time of good health, blessings, and much deserved success.

Masculine Energy
A male relative or friend may be in need of your support or guidance.

Capricorn
Climb Every Mountain
It's time to be the mountain goat and begin your ascent.

Humble Pie
Your ego is strong enough to survive a healthy dose of constructive criticism.

House Card

GO DEEPER, LEARN MORE!

The Sun is the heart center of the chart. When it is in the sign of Capricorn, it activates my

_____ House, which governs _____

_____. When

this House is activated by the Sun, this area of experience will be illuminated. One sentence

to describe how I can make the most of this energy is _____

_____.

Example: If, when the Sun is in Capricorn, it falls in your 5th House, it will illuminate all 5th House issues: the need to socialize, the need to express yourself, the desire to compete in sports, etc. So, make time to explore these activities while this area is illuminated.

Read more about the energies of the Sun, Capricorn, and this House in Heather Arielle's Guidebook for The Fundamentals of Astrology.

January

1 Wednesday

2 Thursday

3 Friday   *Mars enters Sagittarius 4:37 AM*

4 Saturday

5 Sunday

Weekly Inspiration: "Inspire and prepare me for the week."

6 Monday

7 Tuesday

8 Wednesday | January
_____

9 Thursday
_____

10 Friday   *Full Moon Penumbral Lunar Eclipse in Cancer 2:21 PM*
_____

11 Saturday
_____

12 Sunday
_____
Weekly Inspiration: "Inspire and prepare me for the week."

13 Monday   *Venus enters Pisces 1:39 PM*
_____

14 Tuesday
_____

15 Wednesday | January

16 Thursday
Mercury enters Aquarius 1:31 PM

17 Friday

18 Saturday

19 Sunday
Weekly Inspiration: "Inspire and prepare me for the week."

20 Monday
Sun enters Aquarius 9:55 AM (see page 13)

21 Tuesday

Aquarius
To Thine Own Self Be True

No one sees the world quite the way you do.
Celebrate your unique voice & one-of-a-kind style.

Rebel With a Cause

Channel your desire to go against the grain.
Join a humanitarian group or start one yourself.

Aquarius

On January 20, the Sun moves into Aquarius, the eleventh Sign of the Zodiac, and remains there until February 18. The traditional and adult energy of Capricorn is transformed into the unconventional and rebellious energy of Aquarius.

Planet: Uranus, co-ruler Saturn
House: Eleventh
Element: Air
Modality: Fixed

Uranus

IN BALANCE: In balance, Aquarians are champions of the underdog and relentlessly pursue humanitarian causes. In other words, an in-balance Aquarian is a rebel with a cause.

OUT OF BALANCE: Out of balance, Aquarians are still rebellious; only, alas, they tend to lose sight of their cause.

Sun in Aquarius

JANUARY 20, 2020

GO DEEPER, LEARN MORE!

The Sun is the heart center of the chart. When it is in the Sign of Aquarius, it activates my

_____ House, which governs _____

_____. When

this House is activated by the Sun, this area of experience will be illuminated. One sentence

to describe how I can make the most of this energy is _____

_____

_____.

Read more about the energies of the Sun, Aquarius, and this House in Heather Arielle's Guidebook for
The Fundamentals of Astrology.

22 Wednesday | January

23 Thursday

24 Friday   *New Moon in Aquarius 4:42 PM (see page 19)*

25 Saturday

26 Sunday

Weekly Inspiration: "Inspire and prepare me for the week."

27 Monday

28 Tuesday

New Moon Oracle Spread

The two weeks between a New and Full moon is a wonderful time to begin new things. Whatever you start will grow and blossom! Perform the New Moon Oracle Spread each month to learn which energies will be most beneficial to bring into your life during a particular New Moon phase.

Instructions

Separate the cards into categories indicated by the border color, and place in piles.

- The 4 Element cards have melon borders.
- The 3 Modality cards have dark green borders.
- The 11 Planet cards have light blue borders.
- The 12 Zodiac Sign cards have purple borders.
- The 12 House cards have light green borders.

You will not need the other cards for this spread.

CREATE YOUR SPREAD

Card 1: Place the Reversed Moon card.
Card 2: Select one Element card.
Card 3: Select one Modality card.
Card 4: Select one Planet card.
Card 5: Select one Zodiac Sign card.
Card 6: Select one House Card.

```
            ┌──────────┐
            │ Card 1   │
            │(Reversed │
            │  Moon)   │
            └──────────┘
       ┌──────────┐┌──────────┐
       │ Card 2   ││ Card 3   │
       │(element) ││(modality)│
       └──────────┘└──────────┘
   ┌──────────┐┌──────────┐┌──────────┐
   │ Card 4   ││ Card 5   ││ Card 6   │
   │(planet)  ││ (sign)   ││ (house)  │
   └──────────┘└──────────┘└──────────┘
```

Record and Interpret Your Spread

Card 1: The Moon is the most intricate celestial body to master and is mythically connected to the Roman goddess Diana/Greek goddess Artemis. Its receptive qualities often mask its true meaning. The Reversed Card Message, "I Can See Clearly Now" is especially appropriate for New Moon energy. After all, "The fog is lifting. You'll soon have the answers you need to make an informed decision."

Card 2: The Element to incorporate during this New Moon phase is _____.

Two qualities of this Element that I'm being encouraged to embrace are _____

_____.

Card 3: The Modality to incorporate is _____.

Two qualities of this Modality that I'm being inspired to embrace are _____

_____.

Card 4: The Planet's energies to incorporate is _____.

Two qualities of this Planet that I can embrace are _____

_____.

Card 5: The Zodiac Sign that will be of most benefit to me right now is _____.

Three qualities represented by this Sign are _____

_____.

Is there **someone close to me** that resonates to the energy of this Sign? If so, who? _____

_____.

Card 6: The House that will be of most benefit is the _____ House. The area of experience represented by this House is _____

_____

Some activities I can do or actions I can take to activate the energy in this House are _____

_____.

Putting It All Together

Is there a theme? What do you think is the overall message of this New Moon spread?

29 Wednesday | January

30 Thursday

31 Friday

February

1 Saturday

2 Sunday

Weekly Inspiration: "Inspire and prepare me for the week."

3 Monday

Mercury enters Pisces 6:37 AM (see page 23)

4 Tuesday

5 Wednesday

6 Thursday

7 Friday

Venus enters Aries 3:02 PM (see page 23)

MERCURY IN PISCES (FEB 3)

Mercury rules communication, short-distance travel, siblings, and youth. When it is in the Zodiac Sign of Pisces, it is the perfect time to express your sensitive side, explore artistic endeavors, and reach higher levels of consciousness using verbal and communication skills.

GO DEEPER, LEARN MORE!

When Mercury is in the Sign of Pisces, it activates my _____

House, which governs _____

_____

One sentence to describe this aspect for me personally is _____

_____

_____

VENUS IN ARIES (FEB 7)

Venus rules love, relationships, money, and art. When it is in the independent Zodiac Sign of Aries, it is the perfect time to passionately pursue pioneering partnerships and work to bring a higher level of adventure into your existing ones.

GO DEEPER, LEARN MORE!

When Venus is in the Sign of Aries, it activates my _____

House, which governs _____

_____

One sentence to describe this aspect for me personally is _____

_____

_____

Read more about the energies of Mercury, Venus, Pisces, Aries, and these Houses in Heather Arielle's Guidebook for The Fundamentals of Astrology.

8 Saturday | February
_____

9 Sunday   *Full Moon in Leo 2:33 AM*
_____
                    Weekly Inspiration: "Inspire and prepare me for the week."

10 Monday
_____

11 Tuesday
_____

12 Wednesday
_____

13 Thursday
_____

14 Friday
_____

15 Saturday | February

16 Sunday

Mars enters Capricorn 6:33 AM (see page 26)
Mercury Retrograde in Pisces 7:54 PM (see page 27)

Weekly Inspiration: "Inspire and prepare me for the week."

17 Monday

18 Tuesday

Sun enters Pisces 11:57 PM (see pages 29 & 30)

19 Wednesday

20 Thursday

21 Friday

MARS IN CAPRICORN (FEB 16)

Mars is the planet of action, sexuality, sports, and war. When it is in the hard-working Zodiac Sign of Capricorn, it's time to roll up your sleeves and put in those extra hours, if need be, to get the job done. Do this and you will reach your goals.

GO DEEPER, LEARN MORE!

When Mars is in the Sign of Capricorn, it activates my _____ House, which governs

_____.

One sentence to describe this aspect for me personally is _____

_____.

Read more about the energies of Mars, Capricorn, and this House in Heather Arielle's Guidebook for The Fundamentals of Astrology.

Mercury Retrograde Oracle Spread

Reimagine, Reignite, Rejuvenate

Perform this spread whenever Mercury is Retrograde, which occurs several times a year. It will help you focus on the areas ruled by Mercury (writing, thinking, learning, and communicating of all kinds) that are in most need of reflection and review.

*The most important thing to remember about ALL retrogrades is how the word begins—*RE*. And every word that begins with these magical two letters is not just your friend, but your best friend. If you can *RE* it—you can do it!

CREATE YOUR SPREAD

- Place the Upright Mercury Retrograde card in what will be the Center card position.
- Shuffle the remaining cards.
- Creating a 5-pointed star, place the cards in a circle around the Center card, starting with the top-right position.

Card 1:   Area of reflection.
Card 2:   Area of reconnection.
Card 3:   Area to reignite.
Card 4:   Area of refinement.
Card 5:   Path to rejuvenation.

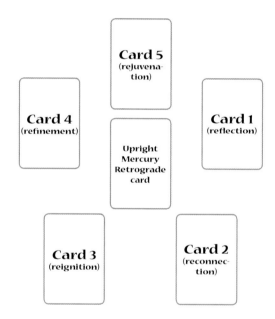

Record and Interpret Your Spread

Once you've completed the spread, fill in the card for each area.

1. Focus of reflection: _____

2. Area of reconnection: _____

3. Area to reignite: _____

4. Area to refine: _____

5. Path to rejuvenation: _____

For each card, describe its inspirational meaning in one sentence.

1. _____

2. _____

3. _____

4. _____

5. _____

Putting It All Together

Is there a theme? What do you think is the overall message of this Mercury Retrograde spread?

Excited about your spread? We love seeing how others use our cards! Tag us with **#houseofastrology** on Social Media and we will share with our online community.

Neptune
A Psychic Gateway Has Opened

Quiet your mind and connect to your guides.
Honor what you hear.

Know Your Boundaries
You or someone close to you may be crossing boundaries that should be observed.

Twelfth House
Take a Slow Boat and Dream

Peaceful, tranquil energy gently envelops you.
Enjoy your solitude.

Secret Knowledge
A secret may soon be revealed. Ask your guides to help bring this hidden knowledge to light.

Water
I Second That Emotion

Your emotions are awakening. Feel the full force of your compassion and empathy.

Shake It Off
Absorbing too much negative energy?
Get out of the water and dry yourself off.

Mutable
Survival of the Fittest

A new approach may be the solution.
Be flexible and adapt!

Jack-of-all-Trades, Master of None
It's time for the dunness to stop changing course. Choose and commit!

Pisces
Get Creative!

Poetic, visionary energy surrounds you. Embrace your inner muse. Let your imagination soar!

Get Moving!

Stimulate your lymphatic system to remove toxins. Walking, swimming, and yoga will all do the trick.

Pisces

On February 18, the Sun moves into Pisces, the twelfth and final Sign of the Zodiac, and remains there until March 19. The rebellious and unconventional energy of Aquarius is transmuted into the intuitive and otherworldly energy of Pisces.

> Planets: Neptune and co-ruler Jupiter
> House: Twelfth
> Element: Water
> Modality: Mutable

Neptune

IN BALANCE: In balance, Pisces individuals do not settle for ordinary outcomes, but instead always strive to reach the ideal.

OUT OF BALANCE: Out of balance, Pisceans blur the line between imagination and fantasy, getting so lost in the latter, they sometimes fail to manifest their gifts in the real world.

Sun in Pisces
FEBRUARY 18, 2020

GO DEEPER, LEARN MORE!

The Sun is the heart center of the chart. When it is in the Sign of Pisces, it activates my

_____ House, which governs _____

_____. When

this House is activated by the Sun, this area of experience will be illuminated. One sentence

to describe how I can make the most of this energy is _____

_____

_____.

> **TIP:** Take a picture of your spread, print it out, and hang it on your refrigerator
> so you can refer to it throughout the month.

22 Saturday | February

23 Sunday

New Moon in Pisces 10:32 AM (see page 32)

Weekly Inspiration: "Inspire and prepare me for the week."

24 Monday

25 Tuesday

26 Wednesday

27 Thursday

28 Friday

29 Saturday

New Moon Oracle Spread

The two weeks between a New and Full moon is a wonderful time to begin new things. Whatever you start will grow and blossom! Perform the New Moon Oracle Spread each month to learn which energies will be most beneficial to bring into your life during a particular New Moon phase.

Instructions

Separate the cards into categories indicated by the border color, and place in piles.

- The 4 Element cards have melon borders.
- The 3 Modality cards have dark green borders.
- The 11 Planet cards have light blue borders.
- The 12 Zodiac Sign cards have purple borders.
- The 12 House cards have light green borders.

You will not need the other cards for this spread.

CREATE YOUR SPREAD

Card 1:   Place the Reversed Moon card.
Card 2:   Select one Element card.
Card 3:   Select one Modality card.
Card 4:   Select one Planet card.
Card 5:   Select one Zodiac Sign card.
Card 6:   Select one House Card.

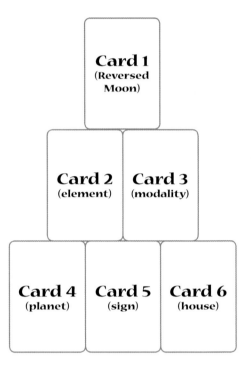

Record and Interpret Your Spread

Card 1: The Moon is the most intricate celestial body to master and is mythically connected to the Roman goddess Diana/Greek goddess Artemis. Its receptive qualities often mask its true meaning. The Reversed Card Message, "I Can See Clearly Now" is especially appropriate for New Moon energy. After all, "The fog is lifting. You'll soon have the answers you need to make an informed decision."

Card 2: The Element to incorporate during this New Moon phase is _____.

Two qualities of this Element that I'm being encouraged to embrace are _____

_____

Card 3: The Modality to incorporate is _____

Two qualities of this Modality that I'm being inspired to embrace are _____

_____

Card 4: The Planet's energies to incorporate is_____.

Two qualities of this Planet that I can embrace are _____

_____.

Card 5: The Zodiac Sign that will be of most benefit to me right now is _____.

Three qualities represented by this Sign are _____

_____.

Is there **someone close to me** that resonates to the energy of this Sign? If so, who? _____

_____.

Card 6: The House that will be of most benefit is the _____ House. The area of experi-

ence represented by this House is _____

_____.

Some activities I can do or actions I can take to activate the energy in this House are _____

_____.

Putting It All Together
Is there a theme? What do you think is the overall message of this New Moon spread?

To make the most of this oracle spread, watch
"New Moon Astrology Oracle Card Spread by Heather Arielle" on YouTube.

March

1 Sunday

Weekly Inspiration: "Inspire and prepare me for the week."

2 Monday

3 Tuesday

4 Wednesday

Mercury Retrograde enters Aquarius 6:07 AM
Venus enters Taurus 10:07 PM (see page 35)

5 Thursday

6 Friday

7 Saturday

VENUS IN TAURUS (MAR 4)

Venus rules love, relationships, money, and art. When Venus is in Taurus, the Sign that it rules, it is the perfect time to explore your most sensual side in your romantic relationships and create partnerships of all kinds that can endure. Concerning money, Taurus encourages financial abundance, so pursue financial ideas in a tangible way and you will prosper.

GO DEEPER, LEARN MORE!

When Venus is in the Sign of Taurus, it activates my _____ House, which governs

_____.

One sentence to describe this aspect for me personally is _____

_____.

Read more about the energies of Venus, Taurus, and this House in Heather Arielle's Guidebook for The Fundamentals of Astrology.

8 Sunday | March

Weekly Inspiration: "Inspire and prepare me for the week."

9 Monday

Full Moon in Virgo 1:48 PM

10 Tuesday

Mercury Direct in Aquarius 11:49 PM

11 Wednesday

12 Thursday

13 Friday

14 Saturday

15 Sunday | March

Weekly Inspiration: "Inspire and prepare me for the week."

16 Monday

Mercury enters Pisces 3:42 AM (see page 38)

17 Tuesday

18 Wednesday

19 Thursday

Sun enters Aries 11:49 PM (see pages 39 & 40)

20 Friday

21 Saturday

MERCURY IN PISCES (MAR 16)

Mercury rules communication, short-distance travel, siblings, and youth. When it is in the Zodiac Sign of Pisces, it is the perfect time to express your sensitive side, explore artistic endeavors, and reach higher levels of consciousness using verbal and communication skills.

GO DEEPER, LEARN MORE!

When Mercury is in the Sign of Pisces, it activates my _____ House, which governs

_____.

One sentence to describe this aspect for me personally is _____

_____.

Read more about these energies in Heather Arielle's Guidebook for The Fundamentals of Astrology.

Mars
Get Physical!

First House
DIY Time

Fire
Ready To Launch

Cardinal
You're Gonna Make It After All

Aries
New Beginnings

Actions you take now will yield swift results.
Charge ahead with your visionary plans.

Patience Is a Virtue

Take your time and follow through
with your pioneering plans.

Aries

On March 19, the Sun moves into Aries, the first Sign of the Western Zodiac, and remains there until April 19. Each year, spring is ushered in with help from this fiery friend. A cardinal Sign, Aries represents powerful new beginnings.

    Planet: Mars
    House: First
    Element: Fire
    Modality: Cardinal

Mars

IN BALANCE: In balance, Aries natives are innovative self-starters, full of productive, fiery energy and fearless in the pursuit of their individual passions.

OUT OF BALANCE: Out of balance, they can lack the patience it takes to stick with an idea or project long enough to see it reach a successful conclusion.

Sun in Aries

MARCH 19, 2020

GO DEEPER, LEARN MORE!

The Sun is the heart center of the chart. When it is in the Sign of Aries, it activates my

_____ House, which governs _____

_____. When

this House is activated by the Sun, this area of experience will be illuminated. One sentence

to describe how I can make the most of this energy is _____

_____

_____.

Read more about the energies of the Sun, Aries, and this House in Heather Arielle's Guidebook for The Fundamentals of Astrology.

22 Sunday | March

Weekly Inspiration: "Inspire and prepare me for the week."

23 Monday

24 Tuesday

New Moon in Aries 5:28 AM (see page 42)

25 Wednesday

26 Thursday

27 Friday

28 Saturday

New Moon Oracle Spread

The two weeks between a New and Full moon is a wonderful time to begin new things. Whatever you start will grow and blossom! Perform the New Moon Oracle Spread each month to learn which energies will be most beneficial to bring into your life during a particular New Moon phase.

Instructions

Separate the cards into categories indicated by the border color, and place in piles.

- The 4 Element cards have melon borders.
- The 3 Modality cards have dark green borders.
- The 11 Planet cards have light blue borders.
- The 12 Zodiac Sign cards have purple borders.
- The 12 House cards have light green borders.

You will not need the other cards for this spread.

CREATE YOUR SPREAD

Card 1: Place the Reversed Moon card.
Card 2: Select one Element card.
Card 3: Select one Modality card.
Card 4: Select one Planet card.
Card 5: Select one Zodiac Sign card.
Card 6: Select one House Card.

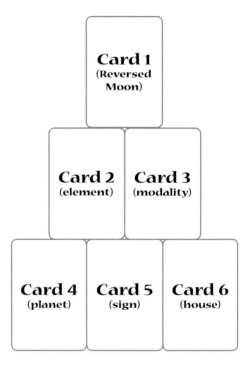

Record and Interpret Your Spread

Card 1: The Moon is the most intricate celestial body to master and is mythically connected to the Roman goddess Diana/Greek goddess Artemis. Its receptive qualities often mask its true meaning. The Reversed Card Message, "I Can See Clearly Now" is especially appropriate for New Moon energy. After all, "The fog is lifting. You'll soon have the answers you need to make an informed decision."

Card 2: The Element to incorporate during this New Moon phase is _____.

Two qualities of this Element that I'm being encouraged to embrace are _____

_____

Card 3: The Modality to incorporate is _____.

Two qualities of this Modality that I'm being inspired to embrace are _____

_____

Card 4: The Planet's energies to incorporate is_____.

Two qualities of this Planet that I can embrace are _____

_____.

Card 5: The Zodiac Sign that will be of most benefit to me right now is _____.

Three qualities represented by this Sign are _____

_____.

Is there **someone close to me** that resonates to the energy of this Sign? If so, who? _____

_____.

Card 6: The House that will be of most benefit is the _____ House. The area of experience represented by this House is _____

_____.

Some activities I can do or actions I can take to activate the energy in this House are _____

_____.

Putting It All Together
Is there a theme? What do you think is the overall message of this New Moon spread?

To make the most of this oracle spread, watch the YouTube video
"New Moon Astrology Oracle Card Spread by Heather Arielle".

29 Sunday | March

Weekly Inspiration: "Inspire and prepare me for the week."

30 Monday

Mars enters Aquarius 3:43 PM (see below)

31 Tuesday

MARS IN AQUARIUS (MAR 30)

Mars is the planet of action, sexuality, sports, and war. When it is in the Zodiac Sign of Aquarius, it's time to actively pursue humanitarian and group endeavors. Mars in Aquarius reminds us that we are all in this together, and only together can we truly move forward in life.

GO DEEPER, LEARN MORE!

When Mars is in the Sign of Aquarius, it activates my _____

House, which governs _____

_____.

One sentence to describe this aspect for me personally is _____

_____

_____

Read more about the energies of Mars, Aquarius, and this House in Heather Arielle's Guidebook for The Fundamentals of Astrology.

April

1 Wednesday

2 Thursday

3 Friday   *Venus enters Gemini 1:10 PM (see page 46)*

4 Saturday

5 Sunday

Weekly Inspiration: "Inspire and prepare me for the week."

6 Monday

7 Tuesday   *Full Moon in Libra 10:35 PM*

VENUS IN GEMINI (APR 3)

Venus rules love, relationships, money, and art. When it is in the Zodiac Sign of Gemini, it's time to explore the more playful side of your partnerships. So flirt, have fun, and be open to introducing new ideas and activities into your most valued relationships.

GO DEEPER, LEARN MORE!

When Venus is in the Sign of Gemini, it activates my _____ House, which governs

_____.

One sentence to describe this aspect for me personally is _____

_____.

Read more about the energies of Venus, Gemini, and this House in Heather Arielle's Guidebook for The Fundamentals of Astrology.

8 Wednesday | April

9 Thursday

10 Friday

11 Saturday   *Mercury enters Aries 12:48 AM (see page 48)*

12 Sunday

Weekly Inspiration: "Inspire and prepare me for the week."

13 Monday

14 Tuesday

Mercury
The Messenger

Your verbal skills are at their peak, so put them to good use. Pen that novel or write that letter!

Something To Talk About
Use your verbal skills to heal old wounds. Your power now lies within your words, so choose them wisely.

Aries
New Beginnings

Actions you take now will yield swift results. Charge ahead with your visionary plans.

Patience Is a Virtue
Take your time and follow through with your pioneering plans.

MERCURY IN ARIES (APR 11)

Mercury rules communication, short-distance travel, siblings, and youth. When it is in the fast-moving Zodiac Sign of Aries, it is the perfect time to passionately pursue your most pioneering ideas. Fast and forceful communication is favored.

GO DEEPER, LEARN MORE!

When Mercury is in the Sign of Aries, it activates my _____ House, which governs

_____.

One sentence to describe this aspect for me personally is _____

_____.

Read more about the energies of Mercury, Aries, and this House in Heather Arielle's Guidebook for The Fundamentals of Astrology.

15 Wednesday | April

16 Thursday

17 Friday

18 Saturday

19 Sunday   *Sun enters Taurus 10:45 AM (see pages 50 & 51)*

Weekly Inspiration: "Inspire and prepare me for the week."

20 Monday

21 Tuesday

Taurus
Cornucopia of Riches

Be tenacious. You have the stamina to manifest your dreams.

You or someone close to you may be trying to control the situation.

No Bullies Allowed!

Taurus

On April 19, the Sun moves into Taurus, the second Sign of the Zodiac, and remains there until May 20. The swift and impulsive energy of Aries is transformed into the enduring and stable energy of Taurus.

> Planet: Venus
> House: Second
> Element: Earth
> Modality: Fixed

IN BALANCE: In balance, Taurus natives demonstrate a resilient tenacity when pursuing a specific goal.

Venus

OUT OF BALANCE: Out of balance, the love Taurus natives have for earthly pleasures can lead to overindulgence and sometimes addictions. Yes, you can have too much of a good thing.

Sun in Taurus

APRIL 19, 2020

GO DEEPER, LEARN MORE!

The Sun is the heart center of the chart. When it is in the Sign of Taurus, it activates my

_____ House, which governs _____

_____. When

this House is activated by the Sun, this area of experience will be illuminated. One sentence

to describe how I can make the most of this energy is _____

_____

_____.

Read more about the energies of the Sun, Taurus, and this House in Heather Arielle's Guidebook for
The Fundamentals of Astrology.

22 Wednesday | April   *New Moon in Taurus 10:26 PM (see page 53)*

23 Thursday

24 Friday

25 Saturday

26 Sunday

Weekly Inspiration: "Inspire and prepare me for the week."

27 Monday   *Mercury enters Taurus 3:53 PM (see page 55)*

28 Tuesday

New Moon Oracle Spread

The two weeks between a New and Full moon is a wonderful time to begin new things. Whatever you start will grow and blossom! Perform the New Moon Oracle Spread each month to learn which energies will be most beneficial to bring into your life during a particular New Moon phase.

Instructions

Separate the cards into categories indicated by the border color, and place in piles.

- The 4 Element cards have melon borders.
- The 3 Modality cards have dark green borders.
- The 11 Planet cards have light blue borders.
- The 12 Zodiac Sign cards have purple borders.
- The 12 House cards have light green borders.

You will not need the other cards for this spread.

CREATE YOUR SPREAD

Card 1: Place the Reversed Moon card.
Card 2: Select one Element card.
Card 3: Select one Modality card.
Card 4: Select one Planet card.
Card 5: Select one Zodiac Sign card.
Card 6: Select one House Card.

```
          ┌──────────┐
          │ Card 1   │
          │(Reversed │
          │  Moon)   │
          └──────────┘
     ┌──────────┐┌──────────┐
     │ Card 2   ││ Card 3   │
     │(element) ││(modality)│
     └──────────┘└──────────┘
┌────────┐┌────────┐┌────────┐
│ Card 4 ││ Card 5 ││ Card 6 │
│(planet)││ (sign) ││(house) │
└────────┘└────────┘└────────┘
```

Record and Interpret Your Spread

Card 1: The Moon is the most intricate celestial body to master and is mythically connected to the Roman goddess Diana/Greek goddess Artemis. Its receptive qualities often mask its true meaning. The Reversed Card Message, "I Can See Clearly Now" is especially appropriate for New Moon energy. After all, "The fog is lifting. You'll soon have the answers you need to make an informed decision."

Card 2: The Element to incorporate during this New Moon phase is _____.

Two qualities of this Element that I'm being encouraged to embrace are _____

_____.

Card 3: The Modality to incorporate is _____.

Two qualities of this Modality that I'm being inspired to embrace are _____

_____.

Card 4: The Planet's energies to incorporate is_____.

Two qualities of this Planet that I can embrace are _____

_____.

Card 5: The Zodiac Sign that will be of most benefit to me right now is _____.

Three qualities represented by this Sign are _____

_____.

Is there **someone close to me** that resonates to the energy of this Sign? If so, who? _____

_____.

Card 6: The House that will be of most benefit is the _____ House. The area of experi-

ence represented by this House is _____

_____

Some activities I can do or actions I can take to activate the energy in this House are _____

_____.

Putting It All Together
Is there a theme? What do you think is the overall message of this New Moon spread?

30 Thursday

MERCURY IN TAURUS (APR 27)

Mercury rules communication, short-distance travel, siblings, and youth. When it is in the slow-moving Zodiac Sign of Taurus, it is the perfect time to develop your practical ideas with patience and persistence. Slow and steady communication is favored.

GO DEEPER, LEARN MORE!

When Mercury is in the Sign of Taurus, it activates my _____

House, which governs _____

_____

One sentence to describe this aspect for me personally is _____

_____

_____

Read more about the energies of Mercury, Taurus, and this Houses in Heather Arielle's Guidebook for The Fundamentals of Astrology.

May

1 Friday

2 Saturday

3 Sunday

Weekly Inspiration: "Inspire and prepare me for the week."

4 Monday

5 Tuesday

6 Wednesday

7 Thursday   *Full Moon in Scorpio 6:45 AM*

8 Friday | May

9 Saturday

10 Sunday

Weekly Inspiration: "Inspire and prepare me for the week."

11 Monday

Mercury enters Gemini 5:58 PM (see page 58)

12 Tuesday

13 Wednesday

Mars enters Pisces 12:17 AM (see page 58)
Venus Retrograde in Gemini 2:45 AM (see page 59)

14 Thursday

MERCURY IN GEMINI (MAY 11)

Mercury rules communication, short-distance travel, siblings, and youth. When it is in Gemini, the Sign that it rules, thinking will be at its most adaptable and curious. Time to learn something new or teach what you already know. Communication of all kinds is especially favored now, so write that novel or set up that coffee date.

GO DEEPER, LEARN MORE!

When Mercury is in the Sign of Gemini, it activates my _____

House, which governs _____

_____

One sentence to describe this aspect for me personally is _____

_____

_____

MARS IN PISCES (MAY 13)

Mars is the planet of action, sexuality, sports, and war. When it is in the Zodiac Sign of Pisces, it's an ideal time to actively pursue artistic and transcendent activities—a time when spiritual warriors come to life.

GO DEEPER, LEARN MORE!

When Mars is in the Sign of Pisces, it activates my _____

House, which governs _____

_____

One sentence to describe this aspect for me personally is _____

_____

_____

Read more about these energies in Heather Arielle's Guidebook for The Fundamentals of Astrology.

Venus Retrograde Oracle Spread

Relationship Review

Perform this spread whenever Venus is Retrograde, which is approximately every eighteen months. It will help you focus on the areas governed by Venus (relationships, money, art) that are in most need of reviewing.

*The most important thing to remember about ALL retrogrades is how the word begins—*RE*. And every word that begins with these magical two letters is not just your friend, but your best friend. If you can *RE* it—you can do it!

CREATE YOUR SPREAD

- Place the Upright Venus Retrograde card in what will be the Center card position.
- Shuffle the remaining cards.
- Creating a 5-pointed star, place the cards in a circle around the Venus Retrograde card, starting with the top-right position.

Card 1: Shows the focus of your reflection concerning your relationships in general.
Card 2: Highlights a relationship that would benefit from a reconnection.
Card 3: Reveals a way to reignite a relationship.
Card 4: Reveals an area in your relationships to refine.
Card 5: Offers a path to rejuvenate your relationships.

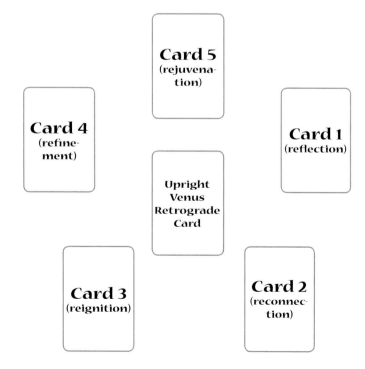

Record and Interpret Your Spread

Once you've completed the spread, fill in the card for each area.

1. Focus of reflection: _____

2. Area of reconnection: _____

3. Way to reignite: _____

4. Area to refine: _____

5. Path to rejuvenation: _____

For each card, describe its inspirational meaning in one sentence.

1. _____

2. _____

3. _____

4. _____

5. _____

Putting It All Together

Is there a theme? What do you think is the overall message of this Venus Retrograde spread?

15 Friday | May

16 Saturday

17 Sunday

Weekly Inspiration: "Inspire and prepare me for the week."

18 Monday

19 Tuesday

20 Wednesday

Sun enters Gemini 9:49 AM (see pages 62 & 63)

21 Thursday

Gemini
Young at Heart

Release your inner child and rediscover your wondrous sense of play!

Call to Action

Stop overthinking the situation and set your plans in motion.

Gemini

On May 20, the Sun moves into Gemini, the third Sign of the Zodiac, and remains there until June 20. The fixed, tenacious energy of Taurus is transformed into the mutable, ever-changing energy of Gemini—they're not called mercurial for nothing.

> Planet: Mercury
> House: Third
> Element: Air
> Modality: Mutable

Mercury

IN BALANCE: In balance, Geminis are playful, witty, and intellectually curious. They excel in communication of all kinds.

OUT OF BALANCE: Out of balance, the ability to see both sides of an issue can spiral into the inability to make a decision, which, yes, even Geminis must do some of the time.

Sun in Gemini

MAY 20, 2020

GO DEEPER, LEARN MORE!

The Sun is the heart center of the chart. When it is in the Sign of Gemini, it activates my

_____ House, which governs _____

_____. When

this House is activated by the Sun, this area of experience will be illuminated. One sentence

to describe how I can make the most of this energy is _____

_____

_____.

Read more about the energies of the Sun, Gemini, and this House in Heather Arielle's Guidebook for The Fundamentals of Astrology.

22 Friday | May   *New Moon in Gemini 1:39 PM (see page 65)*
_____

23 Saturday
_____

24 Sunday
_____
          Weekly Inspiration: "Inspire and prepare me for the week."

25 Monday
_____

26 Tuesday
_____

27 Wednesday
_____

28 Thursday   *Mercury enters Cancer 2:09 PM (see page 67)*
_____

New Moon Oracle Spread

The two weeks between a New and Full moon is a wonderful time to begin new things. Whatever you start will grow and blossom! Perform the New Moon Oracle Spread each month to learn which energies will be most beneficial to bring into your life during a particular New Moon phase.

Instructions

Separate the cards into categories indicated by the border color, and place in piles.

- The 4 Element cards have melon borders.
- The 3 Modality cards have dark green borders.
- The 11 Planet cards have light blue borders.
- The 12 Zodiac Sign cards have purple borders.
- The 12 House cards have light green borders.

You will not need the other cards for this spread.

CREATE YOUR SPREAD

Card 1:   Place the Reversed Moon card.
Card 2:   Select one Element card.
Card 3:   Select one Modality card.
Card 4:   Select one Planet card.
Card 5:   Select one Zodiac Sign card.
Card 6:   Select one House Card.

```
                    ┌─────────────┐
                    │   Card 1    │
                    │ (Reversed   │
                    │   Moon)     │
                    └─────────────┘
              ┌───────────┬───────────┐
              │  Card 2   │  Card 3   │
              │ (element) │ (modality)│
              └───────────┴───────────┘
        ┌──────────┬──────────┬──────────┐
        │ Card 4   │ Card 5   │ Card 6   │
        │ (planet) │ (sign)   │ (house)  │
        └──────────┴──────────┴──────────┘
```

Record and Interpret Your Spread

Card 1: The Moon is the most intricate celestial body to master and is mythically connected to the Roman goddess Diana/Greek goddess Artemis. Its receptive qualities often mask its true meaning. The Reversed Card Message, "I Can See Clearly Now" is especially appropriate for New Moon energy. After all, "The fog is lifting. You'll soon have the answers you need to make an informed decision."

Card 2: The Element to incorporate during this New Moon phase is _____.

Two qualities of this Element that I'm being encouraged to embrace are _____

_____.

Card 3: The Modality to incorporate is _____.

Two qualities of this Modality that I'm being inspired to embrace are _____

_____.

Card 4: The Planet's energies to incorporate is_____.

Two qualities of this Planet that I can embrace are _____

_____.

Card 5: The Zodiac Sign that will be of most benefit to me right now is _____.

Three qualities represented by this Sign are _____

_____.

Is there **someone close to me** that resonates to the energy of this Sign? If so, who? _____

_____.

Card 6: The House that will be of most benefit is the _____ House. The area of experi-

ence represented by this House is _____

_____

Some activities I can do or actions I can take to activate the energy in this House are _____

_____.

Putting It All Together
Is there a theme? What do you think is the overall message of this New Moon spread?

Mercury
The Messenger

Your verbal skills are at their peak, so put them to good use. Pen that novel or write that letter!

Something To Talk About

Use your verbal skills to heal old wounds. Your power now lies within your words, so choose them wisely.

Cancer
Fertility Surrounds You

Nurture your ideas and watch them grow. You are safe and protected on this journey.

The Feminine Mystique

A female friend or relative may be in need of your support or guidance.

MERCURY IN CANCER (MAY 28)

Mercury rules communication, short-distance travel, siblings, and youth. When it is in the sentimental Sign of Cancer, thinking can be especially personal and reflective. Allow the tastes, sounds, and smells of your current environment to transport you back in time; then record your meaningful recollections in a journal.

GO DEEPER, LEARN MORE!

When Mercury is in the Sign of Cancer, it activates my _____ House, which governs

_____.

One sentence to describe this aspect for me personally is _____

_____.

Read more about the energies of Mercury, Cancer, and this House in Heather Arielle's Guidebook for The Fundamentals of Astrology.

29 Friday | May

30 Saturday

31 Sunday

Weekly Inspiration: "Inspire and prepare me for the week."

Share your spread with us! Post to social media and tag us **#houseofastrology**.
It's wonderful to connect in a more personal way!

June

1 Monday

2 Tuesday

3 Wednesday

4 Thursday

5 Friday   *Full Moon Penumbral Lunar Eclipse in Sagittarius 3:12 PM*

6 Saturday

7 Sunday

Weekly Inspiration: "Inspire and prepare me for the week."

8 Monday | June

9 Tuesday

10 Wednesday

11 Thursday

12 Friday

13 Saturday

14 Sunday

Weekly Inspiration: "Inspire and prepare me for the week."

15 Monday | June

16 Tuesday

17 Wednesday

18 Thursday   *Mercury Retrograde in Cancer 12:59 AM (see page 72)*

19 Friday

20 Saturday   *Sun enters Cancer 5:44 PM (see pages 73 & 74)*

21 Sunday   *New Moon Annular Solar Eclipse in Cancer 2:41 AM (see page 76)*

Weekly Inspiration: "Inspire and prepare me for the week."

Mercury Retrograde Oracle Spread

Reimagine, Reignite, Rejuvenate

Perform this spread whenever Mercury is Retrograde, which occurs several times a year. It will help you focus on the areas ruled by Mercury (writing, thinking, learning, and communicating of all kinds) that are in most need of reflection and review.

*The most important thing to remember about ALL retrogrades is how the word begins—*RE*. And every word that begins with these magical two letters is not just your friend, but your best friend. If you can *RE* it—you can do it!

CREATE YOUR SPREAD

- Place the Upright Mercury Retrograde card in what will be the Center card position.
- Shuffle the remaining cards.
- Creating a 5-pointed star, place the cards in a circle around the Center card, starting with the top-right position.

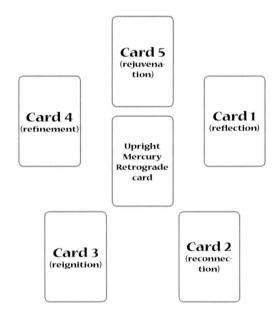

Card 1:   Area of reflection.
Card 2:   Area of reconnection.
Card 3:   Area to reignite.
Card 4:   Area of refinement.
Card 5:   Path to rejuvenation.

Record and Interpret Your Spread

Once you've completed the spread, fill in the card for each area.

1. Focus of reflection: _____

2. Area of reconnection: _____

3. Area to reignite: _____

4. Area to refine: _____

5. Path to rejuvenation: _____

For each card, describe its inspirational meaning in one sentence.

1. _____

2. _____

3. _____

4. _____

5. _____

Putting It All Together

Is there a theme? What do you think is the overall message of this Mercury Retrograde spread?

Excited about your spread? Be sure to post a pic on Instagram and tag us **#houseofastrology.** We'll share with our online community!

Cancer
Fertility Surrounds You

Nurture your ideas and watch them grow.
You are safe and protected on this journey.

The Feminine Mystique

A female friend or relative may be in
need of your support or guidance.

Cancer

On June 20, the Sun moves into Cancer, the fourth Sign of the Zodiac, and remains there until July 22. The detached and childlike energy of Gemini is transformed into the nurturing and protective energy of Cancer.

Planet: Moon
House: Fourth
Element: Water
Modality: Cardinal

Moon

IN BALANCE: In balance, Cancers successfully juggle the need to support and nurture their families without neglecting themselves.

OUT OF BALANCE: Out of balance, Cancers may begin to feel overwhelmed by family duties and responsibilities. Ask yourself, "Am I the only caregiver in my circle? Is someone taking advantage of my innate nurturing gifts?"

Sun in Cancer

JUNE 20, 2019

GO DEEPER, LEARN MORE!

The Sun is the heart center of the chart. When it is in the Sign of Cancer, it activates my

_____ House, which governs _____

_____. When

this House is activated by the Sun, this area of experience will be illuminated. One sentence

to describe how I can make the most of this energy is _____

_____

_____.

Read more about the energies of the Sun, Cancer, and this House in Heather Arielle's Guidebook for The Fundamentals of Astrology.

New Moon Oracle Spread

The two weeks between a New and Full moon is a wonderful time to begin new things. Whatever you start will grow and blossom! Perform the New Moon Oracle Spread each month to learn which energies will be most beneficial to bring into your life during a particular New Moon phase.

Instructions

Separate the cards into categories indicated by the border color, and place in piles.

- The 4 Element cards have melon borders.
- The 3 Modality cards have dark green borders.
- The 11 Planet cards have light blue borders.
- The 12 Zodiac Sign cards have purple borders.
- The 12 House cards have light green borders.

You will not need the other cards for this spread.

CREATE YOUR SPREAD

Card 1: Place the Reversed Moon card.
Card 2: Select one Element card.
Card 3: Select one Modality card.
Card 4: Select one Planet card.
Card 5: Select one Zodiac Sign card.
Card 6: Select one House Card.

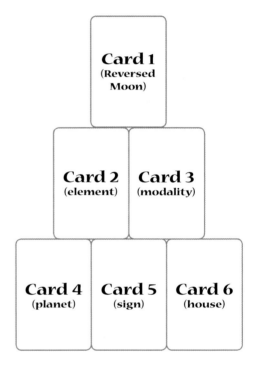

Record and Interpret Your Spread

Card 1: The Moon is the most intricate celestial body to master and is mythically connected to the Roman goddess Diana/Greek goddess Artemis. Its receptive qualities often mask its true meaning. The Reversed Card Message, "I Can See Clearly Now" is especially appropriate for New Moon energy. After all, "The fog is lifting. You'll soon have the answers you need to make an informed decision."

Card 2: The Element to incorporate during this New Moon phase is _____.

Two qualities of this Element that I'm being encouraged to embrace are _____

_____

Card 3: The Modality to incorporate is _____.

Two qualities of this Modality that I'm being inspired to embrace are _____

_____

Card 4: The Planet's energies to incorporate is_____.

Two qualities of this Planet that I can embrace are _____

_____.

Card 5: The Zodiac Sign that will be of most benefit to me right now is _____.

Three qualities represented by this Sign are _____

_____.

Is there **someone close to me** that resonates to the energy of this Sign? If so, who? _____

_____.

Card 6: The House that will be of most benefit is the _____ House. The area of experi-

ence represented by this House is _____

_____.

Some activities I can do or actions I can take to activate the energy in this House are _____

_____.

Putting It All Together
Is there a theme? What do you think is the overall message of this New Moon spread?

22 Monday | June

23 Tuesday

24 Wednesday

25 Thursday   *Venus Direct in Gemini 2:48 AM*

26 Friday

27 Saturday   *Mars enters Aries 9:45 PM (until January 2021, see page 80)*

28 Sunday

Weekly Inspiration: "Inspire and prepare me for the week."

30 Tuesday

MARS IN ARIES (JUNE 27)

Mars is the planet of action, sexuality, sports, and war. When it is in the Zodiac Sign of Aries, the Sign that it rules, the energy of Mars is most easily expressed. Time to charge ahead with your pioneering plans. Adventure travel is also encouraged.

GO DEEPER, LEARN MORE!

When Mars is in the Sign of Aries, it activates my _____

House, which governs _____

_____

One sentence to describe this aspect for me personally is _____

_____

_____

Spotlight on Mars in Aries

JUNE 27, 2020 – JANUARY 7, 2021

Because of a Mars Retrograde, which happens only every couple of years, Mars will remain in the fiery Zodiac Sign of Aries from **June 27 – January 7, 2021**—that's over six months. Mars is the planet of action, sexuality, sports, and war. When it is in Aries, the Sign that it rules, the energy of Mars is most easily expressed. In order to make the most of this extended period of Mars in Aries, it's important to break up this six-month period into three smaller windows of time.

WINDOW ONE: From June 27-September 9, charge ahead with pioneering plans and new beginnings. It's a time to move forward with both projects and relationships.

WINDOW TWO: From September 9-November 13, Mars will be retrograde; and during this period, it will be a time to review and reevaluate the plans, projects, and relationships that you were developing between June 27-September 9. During Mars Retrograde, ask yourself the question, "How much force do I really need to use in this situation or relationship in order to get the result that I want?"

WINDOW THREE: Upon reflection, if you decide that you have been coming on too strong, once Mars goes direct on November 13, you may wish to adopt a gentler approach. If, on the other hand, you decide you've been too passive in the pursuit of your goals, once Mars goes direct, it will be time to assert yourself.

July

1 Wednesday

2 Thursday

3 Friday

4 Saturday

5 Sunday   *Full Moon Penumbral Lunar Eclipse in Capricorn 12:44 AM*

Weekly Inspiration: "Inspire and prepare me for the week."

6 Monday

7 Tuesday

8 Wednesday | July

9 Thursday

10 Friday

11 Saturday

12 Sunday   *Mercury Direct in Cancer 4:26 AM*

                        Weekly Inspiration: "Inspire and prepare me for the week."

13 Monday

14 Tuesday

15 Wednesday | July

16 Thursday

17 Friday

18 Saturday

19 Sunday

Weekly Inspiration: "Inspire and prepare me for the week."

20 Monday

New Moon in Cancer 1:33 PM (see page 84)

21 Tuesday

New Moon Oracle Spread

The two weeks between a New and Full moon is a wonderful time to begin new things. Whatever you start will grow and blossom! Perform the New Moon Oracle Spread each month to learn which energies will be most beneficial to bring into your life during a particular New Moon phase.

Instructions

Separate the cards into categories indicated by the border color, and place in piles.

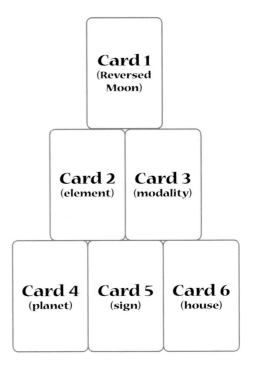

- The 4 Element cards have melon borders.
- The 3 Modality cards have dark green borders.
- The 11 Planet cards have light blue borders.
- The 12 Zodiac Sign cards have purple borders.
- The 12 House cards have light green borders.

You will not need the other cards for this spread.

CREATE YOUR SPREAD

Card 1: Place the Reversed Moon card.
Card 2: Select one Element card.
Card 3: Select one Modality card.
Card 4: Select one Planet card.
Card 5: Select one Zodiac Sign card.
Card 6: Select one House Card.

Record and Interpret Your Spread

Card 1: The Moon is the most intricate celestial body to master and is mythically connected to the Roman goddess Diana/Greek goddess Artemis. Its receptive qualities often mask its true meaning. The Reversed Card Message, "I Can See Clearly Now" is especially appropriate for New Moon energy. After all, "The fog is lifting. You'll soon have the answers you need to make an informed decision."

Card 2: The Element to incorporate during this New Moon phase is _____.

Two qualities of this Element that I'm being encouraged to embrace are _____

_____.

Card 3: The Modality to incorporate is _____

Two qualities of this Modality that I'm being inspired to embrace are _____

_____.

Card 4: The Planet's energies to incorporate is_____.

Two qualities of this Planet that I can embrace are _____

_____.

Card 5: The Zodiac Sign that will be of most benefit to me right now is _____.

Three qualities represented by this Sign are _____

_____.

Is there **someone close to me** that resonates to the energy of this Sign? If so, who? _____

_____.

Card 6: The House that will be of most benefit is the _____ House. The area of experi-

ence represented by this House is _____

_____.

Some activities I can do or actions I can take to activate the energy in this House are _____

_____.

Putting It All Together
Is there a theme? What do you think is the overall message of this New Moon spread?

22 Wednesday | July   *Sun enters Leo 4:37 AM (see pages 87 & 88)*

23 Thursday

24 Friday

25 Saturday

26 Sunday

Weekly Inspiration: "Inspire and prepare me for the week."

27 Monday

28 Tuesday

Sun
Shine Your Light Brightly
Celebrate this time of good health, blessings, and much deserved success.

Masculine Energy
A male source or friend may be in need of your support or guidance.

Fifth House
Romance Is in the Air
Expect old passions to be rekindled; look for new ones to be stoked.

Bringing Up Baby
You're about to give birth to something beautiful. Enjoy your creation!

Fire
Ready To Launch
Be bold and resolute. It is time to take action.

Failure To Launch
Are your energy reserves running low? Take time out to relax and recharge.

Fixed
Hold Fast to Your Dreams
You're capable of intense, prolonged, focused energy. Embrace your passion. You will triumph!

An Adjustment Is Required
This is as new as you're go to an about-face, but you may need to refine your approach.

Leo
Express Yourself

Magical creative energy is all around you.
Lap up the praise & attention—you deserve it!

Oh, Very Young

The answer to your question may involve your child or the child of someone you know.

Leo

On July 22, the Sun moves into Leo, the fifth Sign of the Zodiac, and remains there until August 22. The personal, introverted energy of Cancer is transformed into the outgoing, dramatic energy of Leo.

Planet: Sun
House: Fifth
Element: Fire
Modality: Fixed

Sun

IN BALANCE: In balance, Leos make dynamic, inspirational leaders in whose regal presence anything can seem possible.

OUT OF BALANCE: Out of balance, Leos' naturally high levels of confidence can slip into high levels of arrogance.

Sun in Leo

JULY 22, 2020

Sun
Shine Your Light Brightly
Celebrate this time of good health, blessings, and much deserved success.

Masculine Energy
A male relative or friend may be in need of your support or guidance.

Leo
Express Yourself
Magical creative energy is all around you. Lap up the praise & attention—you deserve it!

Oh, Very Young
The answer to your question may involve your child or the child of someone you know.

House Card

GO DEEPER, LEARN MORE!

The Sun is the heart center of the chart. When it is in the Sign of Leo, it activates my _____ House, which governs _____

_____. When this House is activated by the Sun, this area of experience will be illuminated. One sentence to describe how I can make the most of this energy is _____

_____

_____.

Read more about the energies of the Sun, Leo, and this House in Heather Arielle's Guidebook for The Fundamentals of Astrology.

29 Wednesday | July

_____

30 Thursday

_____

31 Friday

_____

Prepare for the year ahead! Order your 2021 Astrology Oracle Card Planner
in print or as a digital download from AriellesAstrology.com.

August

1 Saturday

2 Sunday

Weekly Inspiration: "Inspire and prepare me for the week."

3 Monday

Full Moon in Aquarius 11:59 AM

4 Tuesday

Mercury enters Leo 11:32 PM (see page 91)

5 Wednesday

6 Thursday

7 Friday

Venus enters Cancer 11:21 AM (see page 91)

MERCURY IN LEO (AUG 4)

Mercury rules communication, short-distance travel, siblings, and youth. When it is in the dramatic Zodiac Sign of Leo, it's the perfect time to express yourself. Communicate your most creative ideas with enthusiasm, and you will gain a loyal following.

GO DEEPER, LEARN MORE!

When Mercury is in the Sign of Leo, it activates my _____

House, which governs _____

_____

One sentence to describe this aspect for me personally is _____

_____

_____

VENUS IN CANCER (AUG 7)

Venus rules love, relationships, money, and art. When it is in the sensitive and personal Zodiac Sign of Cancer, it's a wonderful time to deepen your relationships, especially with family and those who feel like family.

GO DEEPER, LEARN MORE!

When Venus is in the Sign of Cancer, it activates my _____

House, which governs _____

_____

One sentence to describe this aspect for me personally is _____

_____

_____

Read more about the energies of the Planets, Signs, and Houses in Heather Arielle's Guidebook for The Fundamentals of Astrology.

8 Saturday | August

9 Sunday

Weekly Inspiration: "Inspire and prepare me for the week."

10 Monday

11 Tuesday

12 Wednesday

13 Thursday

14 Friday

15 Saturday | August
_____

16 Sunday
_____
Weekly Inspiration: "Inspire and prepare me for the week."

17 Monday
_____

18 Tuesday   *New Moon in Leo 10:42 PM (see page 94)*
_____

19 Wednesday   *Mercury in Virgo 9:35 PM (see page 96)*
_____

20 Thursday
_____

21 Friday
_____

New Moon Oracle Spread

The two weeks between a New and Full moon is a wonderful time to begin new things. Whatever you start will grow and blossom! Perform the New Moon Oracle Spread each month to learn which energies will be most beneficial to bring into your life during a particular New Moon phase.

Instructions

Separate the cards into categories indicated by the border color, and place in piles.

- The 4 Element cards have melon borders.
- The 3 Modality cards have dark green borders.
- The 11 Planet cards have light blue borders.
- The 12 Zodiac Sign cards have purple borders.
- The 12 House cards have light green borders.

You will not need the other cards for this spread.

CREATE YOUR SPREAD

Card 1:   Place the Reversed Moon card.
Card 2:   Select one Element card.
Card 3:   Select one Modality card.
Card 4:   Select one Planet card.
Card 5:   Select one Zodiac Sign card.
Card 6:   Select one House Card.

Record and Interpret Your Spread

Card 1: The Moon is the most intricate celestial body to master and is mythically connected to the Roman goddess Diana/Greek goddess Artemis. Its receptive qualities often mask its true meaning. The Reversed Card Message, "I Can See Clearly Now" is especially appropriate for New Moon energy. After all, "The fog is lifting. You'll soon have the answers you need to make an informed decision."

Card 2: The Element to incorporate during this New Moon phase is _____.

Two qualities of this Element that I'm being encouraged to embrace are _____

_____

Card 3: The Modality to incorporate is _____.

Two qualities of this Modality that I'm being inspired to embrace are _____

_____

Card 4: The Planet's energies to incorporate is_____.

Two qualities of this Planet that I can embrace are _____

_____.

Card 5: The Zodiac Sign that will be of most benefit to me right now is _____.

Three qualities represented by this Sign are _____

_____.

Is there **someone close to me** that resonates to the energy of this Sign? If so, who? _____

_____.

Card 6: The House that will be of most benefit is the _____ House. The area of experi-

ence represented by this House is _____

_____

Some activities I can do or actions I can take to activate the energy in this House are _____

_____.

Putting It All Together
Is there a theme? What do you think is the overall message of this New Moon spread?

Mercury
The Messenger
Your verbal skills are at their peak, so put them to good use. Pen that novel or write that letter!

Something To Talk About
Use your verbal skills to heal old wounds. Your power now lies within your words, so choose them wisely.

Virgo
The World Needs You
Honor your deep desire to be of service to humanity. It's time to leave your mark.

Express Gratitude
Make sure you see the big picture. Your glass is not just half full—it's overflowing!

MERCURY IN VIRGO (AUG 19)

Mercury rules communication, short-distance travel, siblings, and youth. When it is in Virgo, the Sign that it rules, your ability to process and organize vast amounts of information is enhanced. Precise communication is favored; so perfect your thoughts and share them in written forms, whether that be novels, plays, or simple text messages.

GO DEEPER, LEARN MORE!

When Mercury is in the Sign of Virgo, it activates my _____ House, which governs

_____.

One sentence to describe this aspect for me personally is _____

_____.

Read more about the energies of Mercury, Virgo, and this House in Heather Arielle's Guidebook for The Fundamentals of Astrology.

22 Saturday | August *Sun enters Virgo 11:45 AM* *(see pages 98 & 99)*

23 Sunday

Weekly Inspiration: "Inspire and prepare me for the week."

24 Monday

25 Tuesday

26 Wednesday

27 Thursday

28 Friday

Mercury
The Messenger

Your verbal skills are at their peak, so put them to good use. Pen that novel or write that letter!

Something To Talk About

Sixth House
Busy As a Bee

Transform your daily health habits. Fortify your body and boost your immunity.

Animal Crackers

Earth
Indulge Your Senses

Embrace earthly pleasure. Connect to the natural world. Manifesting energy surrounds you.

My Favorite Things

Mutable
Survival of the Fittest

A new approach may be the solution. Be flexible and adapt!

Jack-of-all-Trades Master of None

Virgo
The World Needs You

Honor your deep desire to be of service to humanity. It's time to leave your mark.

Express Gratitude

Make sure you see the big picture. Your glass is not just half full—it's overflowing!

Virgo

On August 22, the Sun moves into Virgo, the sixth Sign of the Zodiac, and remains there until September 22. The dramatic and scene stealing energy of Leo is transmuted into the modest and unassuming energy of Virgo. Ruled by Mercury, Virgo is a discriminating Sign.

Planet: Mercury
House: Sixth
Element: Earth
Modality: Mutable

Mercury

IN BALANCE: In balance, Virgos can reach any goal they set for themselves, propelled by their deep desire to reach perfection. They will not miss a detail when analyzing a complex problem

OUT OF BALANCE: Out of balance, the desire Virgos have to reach perfection and their ability to notice every single detail can unravel into judgmental and self-critical behavior. When this happens, Virgos can become their own worst enemies.

Sun in Virgo
AUGUST 22, 2020

Sun
Shine Your Light Brightly
Celebrate this time of good health, blessings, and much deserved success.

Masculine Energy
A male relative or friend may be in need of your support or guidance.

Virgo
The World Needs You
Honor your deep desire to be of service to humanity. It's time to leave your mark.

Express Gratitude
Make sure you see the big picture. Your glass is not just half full—it's overflowing!

House Card

GO DEEPER, LEARN MORE!

The Sun is the heart center of the chart. When it is in the Sign of Virgo, it activates my

_____ House, which governs _____

_____. When

this House is activated by the Sun, this area of experience will be illuminated. One sentence

to describe how I can make the most of this energy is _____

_____

_____.

Read more about the energies of the Sun, Virgo, and this House in Heather Arielle's Guidebook for The Fundamentals of Astrology.

29 Saturday | August

30 Sunday

Weekly Inspiration: "Inspire and prepare me for the week."

31 Monday

Prepare for the year ahead! Order your 2021 Astrology Oracle Card Planner
in print or as a digital download from AriellesAstrology.com.

September

1 Tuesday

2 Wednesday   *Full Moon in Pisces 1:22 AM*

3 Thursday

4 Friday

5 Saturday   *Mercury enters Libra 3:46 PM (see page 102)*

6 Sunday   *Venus enters Leo 3:21 AM (see page 102)*

Weekly Inspiration: "Inspire and prepare me for the week."

7 Monday

MERCURY IN LIBRA (SEP 5)

Mercury rules communication, short-distance travel, siblings, and youth. When it is in the balanced Sign of Libra, diplomatic communication is favored. So go ahead and gently assert yourself; just make sure when trying to win someone over, you are presenting all sides of an issue.

GO DEEPER, LEARN MORE!

When Mercury is in the Sign of Libra, it activates my _____

House, which governs _____

_____

One sentence to describe this aspect for me personally is _____

_____

_____

VENUS IN LEO (SEP 6)

Venus rules love, relationships, money, and art. When it is in the dramatic Zodiac Sign of Leo, it's the perfect time to socialize. So, say yes to that party, event, date, or opportunity.

GO DEEPER, LEARN MORE!

When Venus is in the Sign of Leo, it activates my _____

House, which governs _____

_____

One sentence to describe this aspect for me personally is _____

_____

_____

Read more about the energies of these Planets, Signs, and Houses in Heather Arielle's Guidebook for The Fundamentals of Astrology.

8 Tuesday | September

9 Wednesday   *Mars Retrograde in Aries 6:22 PM (see page 104)*

10 Thursday

11 Friday

12 Saturday

13 Sunday

Weekly Inspiration: "Inspire and prepare me for the week."

14 Monday

Mars Retrograde Oracle Spread

Rethink How You Use Your Energy

Perform this spread whenever Mars is Retrograde, which is approximately every two years. It will help you focus on the areas ruled by Mars (health, temperament, and ability to take action) that are in most need of revitalization.

The most important thing to remember about ALL retrogrades is how the word begins—*RE*. And every word that begins with these magical two letters is not just your friend, but your best friend. If you can *RE* it—you can do it!

CREATE YOUR SPREAD

- Place the Upright Mars Retrograde card in what will be the Center position.
- Shuffle the remaining cards.
- Creating a 5-pointed star, place the cards in a circle around the Mars Retrograde card, starting with the top-right position.

Card 1: This card shows you the focus of your reflection concerning your temperament.

Card 2: In what ways or areas could you become more assertive?

Card 3: In what areas or situations could you become less assertive?

Card 4: What passion or activity is best for reengaging?

Card 5: How can you best rejuvenate your overall energy?

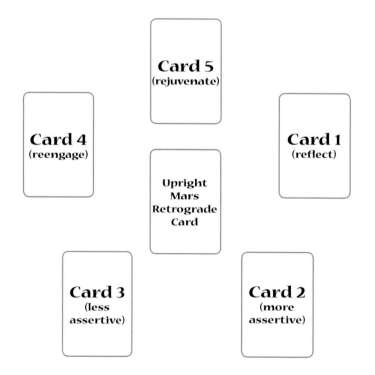

Record and Interpret Your Spread

Once you've completed the spread, fill in the card for each area.

1. Focus of reflection: _____

2. Area to be more assertive: _____

3. Area to be less assertive: _____

4. Area for reengaging: _____

5. Path to rejuvenation: _____

For each card, describe its inspirational meaning in one sentence.

1. _____

2. _____

3. _____

4. _____

5. _____

Putting It All Together

Is there a theme? What do you think is the overall message of this Mars Retrograde spread?

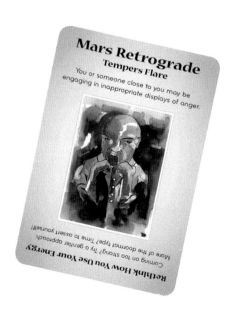

15 Tuesday | September

16 Wednesday

17 Thursday

New Moon in Virgo 7:00 AM (see page 107)

18 Friday

19 Saturday

20 Sunday

Weekly Inspiration: "Inspire and prepare me for the week."

21 Monday

New Moon Oracle Spread

The two weeks between a New and Full moon is a wonderful time to begin new things. Whatever you start will grow and blossom! Perform the New Moon Oracle Spread each month to learn which energies will be most beneficial to bring into your life during a particular New Moon phase.

Instructions

Separate the cards into categories indicated by the border color, and place in piles.

- The 4 Element cards have melon borders.
- The 3 Modality cards have dark green borders.
- The 11 Planet cards have light blue borders.
- The 12 Zodiac Sign cards have purple borders.
- The 12 House cards have light green borders.

You will not need the other cards for this spread.

CREATE YOUR SPREAD

Card 1:   Place the Reversed Moon card.
Card 2:   Select one Element card.
Card 3:   Select one Modality card.
Card 4:   Select one Planet card.
Card 5:   Select one Zodiac Sign card.
Card 6:   Select one House Card.

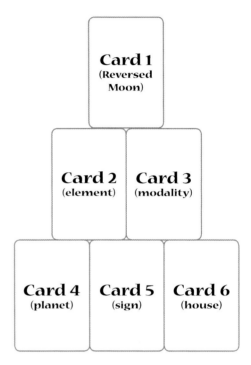

Record and Interpret Your Spread

Card 1: The Moon is the most intricate celestial body to master and is mythically connected to the Roman goddess Diana/Greek goddess Artemis. Its receptive qualities often mask its true meaning. The Reversed Card Message, "I Can See Clearly Now" is especially appropriate for New Moon energy. After all, "The fog is lifting. You'll soon have the answers you need to make an informed decision."

Card 2: The Element to incorporate during this New Moon phase is _____.

Two qualities of this Element that I'm being encouraged to embrace are _____

_____.

Card 3: The Modality to incorporate is _____.

Two qualities of this Modality that I'm being inspired to embrace are _____

_____.

Card 4: The Planet's energies to incorporate is_____.

Two qualities of this Planet that I can embrace are _____

_____.

Card 5: The Zodiac Sign that will be of most benefit to me right now is _____.

Three qualities represented by this Sign are _____

_____.

Is there **someone close to me** that resonates to the energy of this Sign? If so, who? _____

_____.

Card 6: The House that will be of most benefit is the _____ House. The area of experi-

ence represented by this House is _____

_____.

Some activities I can do or actions I can take to activate the energy in this House are _____

_____.

Putting It All Together
Is there a theme? What do you think is the overall message of this New Moon spread?

22 Tuesday | September   *Sun enters Libra 9:30 AM (see pages 110 & 111)*
_____

23 Wednesday
_____

24 Thursday
_____

25 Friday
_____

26 Saturday
_____

27 Sunday   *Mercury enters Scorpio 3:40 AM (see page 112)*
_____
                    Weekly Inspiration: "Inspire and prepare me for the week."

28 Monday
_____

Venus
Open Your Heart to Love

Seventh House
One-on-One

Air
Prick Up Your Ears!

Cardinal
You're Gonna Make It After All

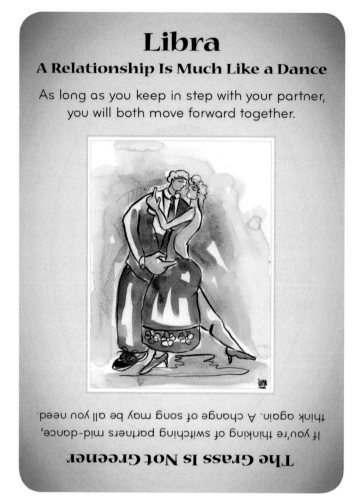

Libra
A Relationship Is Much Like a Dance

As long as you keep in step with your partner, you will both move forward together.

The Grass Is Not Greener

If you're thinking of switching partners mid-dance, think again. A change of song may be all you need.

Libra

On September 22, the Sun moves into Libra, the seventh Sign of the Zodiac, and remains there until October 22. The Virgo desire to be of service to humanity is transformed into the Libra desire to be of service to a partner. Ruled by Venus, Libra governs all types of partnerships, relationships, and collaborations.

> Planet: Venus
> House: Seventh
> Element: Air
> Modality: Cardinal

Venus

IN BALANCE: In balance, Libras make great leaders, their judgments accepted as being fair and impartial. They move projects forward effortlessly using their charm and diplomacy.

OUT OF BALANCE: Out of balance, the desire of Libras to weigh both sides of a situation evenly can spiral into the inability to choose a side or make a decision.

Sun in Libra
SEPTEMBER 22, 2020

GO DEEPER, LEARN MORE!

The Sun is the heart center of the chart. When it is in the Sign of Libra, it activates my

_____ House, which governs _____

_____. When

this House is activated by the Sun, this area of experience will be illuminated. One sentence

to describe how I can make the most of this energy is _____

_____

_____.

Read more about the energies of the Sun, Libra, and this House in Heather Arielle's Guidebook for The Fundamentals of Astrology.

29 Tuesday | September

30 Wednesday

MERCURY IN SCORPIO (SEP 27)

Mercury rules communication, short-distance travel, siblings, and youth. When it is in the intense Zodiac Sign of Scorpio, communication can become secretive and thoughts can become obsessive. Need to know more about a subject? Mercury in Scorpio is an ideal time to dig deep and do the research. Hidden truths can be revealed now.

GO DEEPER, LEARN MORE!

When Mercury is in the Sign of Scorpio, it activates my _____

House, which governs _____

_____

One sentence to describe this aspect for me personally is _____

_____

_____

Read more about the energies of Mercury, Scorpio, and this House in Heather Arielle's Guidebook for The Fundamentals of Astrology.

October

1 Thursday *Full Moon in Aries 5:05 PM*

2 Friday *Venus enters Virgo 4:48 PM (see page 114)*

3 Saturday

4 Sunday

Weekly Inspiration: "Inspire and prepare me for the week."

5 Monday

6 Tuesday

7 Wednesday

Venus
Open Your Heart to Love
Your soul mate is trying to find a way in.

Balance the Budget
Financial discipline and conservative investments are favored at this time.

Virgo
The World Needs You
Honor your deep desire to be of service to humanity. It's time to leave your mark.

Express Gratitude
Make sure you see the big picture. Your glass is not just half full—it's overflowing!

VENUS IN VIRGO (OCT 2)

Venus rules love, relationships, money, and art. When it is in the Zodiac Sign of Virgo, ask yourself, "How can I better be of service to my partner? How can my partner be of better service to me?"

GO DEEPER, LEARN MORE!

When Venus is in the Sign of Virgo, it activates my _____ House, which governs

_____.

One sentence to describe this aspect for me personally is _____

_____.

Read more about the energies of Venus, Virgo, and this House in Heather Arielle's Guidebook for The Fundamentals of Astrology.

8 Thursday | October

9 Friday

10 Saturday

11 Sunday

Weekly Inspiration: "Inspire and prepare me for the week."

12 Monday

13 Tuesday

Mercury Retrograde in Scorpio 9:05 PM (see page 116)

14 Wednesday

Mercury Retrograde Oracle Spread

Reimagine, Reignite, Rejuvenate

Perform this spread whenever Mercury is Retrograde, which occurs several times a year. It will help you focus on the areas ruled by Mercury (writing, thinking, learning, and communicating of all kinds) that are in most need of reflection and review.

*The most important thing to remember about ALL retrogrades is how the word begins—*RE*. And every word that begins with these magical two letters is not just your friend, but your best friend. If you can *RE* it—you can do it!

CREATE YOUR SPREAD

- Place the Upright Mercury Retrograde card in what will be the Center card position.
- Shuffle the remaining cards.
- Creating a 5-pointed star, place the cards in a circle around the Center card, starting with the top-right position.

Card 1: Area of reflection.
Card 2: Area of reconnection.
Card 3: Area to reignite.
Card 4: Area of refinement.
Card 5: Path to rejuvenation.

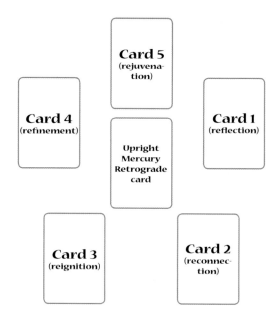

Record and Interpret Your Spread

Once you've completed the spread, fill in the card for each area.

1. Focus of reflection: _____

2. Area of reconnection: _____

3. Area to reignite: _____

4. Area to refine: _____

5. Path to rejuvenation: _____

For each card, describe its inspirational meaning in one sentence.

1. _____

2. _____

3. _____

4. _____

5. _____

Putting It All Together

Is there a theme? What do you think is the overall message of this Mercury Retrograde spread?

15 Thursday | October

16 Friday   *New Moon in Libra 3:31 PM (see page 119)*

17 Saturday

18 Sunday

Weekly Inspiration: "Inspire and prepare me for the week."

19 Monday

20 Tuesday

21 Wednesday

New Moon Oracle Spread

The two weeks between a New and Full moon is a wonderful time to begin new things. Whatever you start will grow and blossom! Perform the New Moon Oracle Spread each month to learn which energies will be most beneficial to bring into your life during a particular New Moon phase.

Instructions

Separate the cards into categories indicated by the border color, and place in piles.

- The 4 Element cards have melon borders.
- The 3 Modality cards have dark green borders.
- The 11 Planet cards have light blue borders.
- The 12 Zodiac Sign cards have purple borders.
- The 12 House cards have light green borders.

You will not need the other cards for this spread.

CREATE YOUR SPREAD

Card 1:   Place the Reversed Moon card.
Card 2:   Select one Element card.
Card 3:   Select one Modality card.
Card 4:   Select one Planet card.
Card 5:   Select one Zodiac Sign card.
Card 6:   Select one House Card.

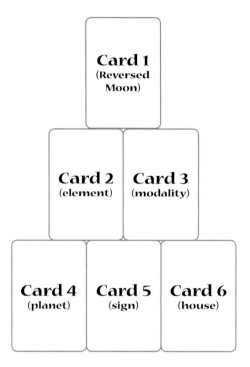

Record and Interpret Your Spread

Card 1: The Moon is the most intricate celestial body to master and is mythically connected to the Roman goddess Diana/Greek goddess Artemis. Its receptive qualities often mask its true meaning. The Reversed Card Message, "I Can See Clearly Now" is especially appropriate for New Moon energy. After all, "The fog is lifting. You'll soon have the answers you need to make an informed decision."

Card 2: The Element to incorporate during this New Moon phase is _____.

Two qualities of this Element that I'm being encouraged to embrace are _____

_____.

Card 3: The Modality to incorporate is _____.

Two qualities of this Modality that I'm being inspired to embrace are _____

_____.

Card 4: The Planet's energies to incorporate is_____.

Two qualities of this Planet that I can embrace are _____

_____.

Card 5: The Zodiac Sign that will be of most benefit to me right now is _____.

Three qualities represented by this Sign are _____

_____.

Is there **someone close to me** that resonates to the energy of this Sign? If so, who? _____

_____.

Card 6: The House that will be of most benefit is the _____ House. The area of experience represented by this House is _____

_____

Some activities I can do or actions I can take to activate the energy in this House are _____

_____.

Putting It All Together
Is there a theme? What do you think is the overall message of this New Moon spread?

22 Thursday | October   *Sun enters Scorpio 6:59 PM (see pages 122 & 123)*

_____

23 Friday

_____

24 Saturday

_____

25 Sunday
_____
            Weekly Inspiration: "Inspire and prepare me for the week."

26 Monday

_____

                            Mercury Retrograde enters Libra 9:33 PM
27 Tuesday   *Venus enters Libra 9:41 PM (see page 124)*

_____

28 Wednesday

_____

Pluto
The Circle of Life

Eighth House
Obsessions Can Be Beautiful

Water
I Second That Emotion

Fixed
Hold Fast to Your Dreams

Scorpio
The Evolution of Man & Woman

Allow transformation to enter your life. You will transform not only yourself, but others as well.

The Phoenix Will Rise

If you've been ill recently, your guides bring you a message of regeneration and healing.

Scorpio

On October 22, the Sun moves into Scorpio, the eighth Sign of the Zodiac, and remains there until November 21. The balanced and refined energy of Libra is transformed into the passionate and possessive energy of Scorpio, the most intense Sign of the Zodiac.

Planet: Pluto, co-ruler Mars
House: Eighth
Element: Water
Modality: Fixed

Pluto

IN BALANCE: In balance, Scorpios are able to use their immense powers to not only transform themselves, but also to transform society for the better.

OUT OF BALANCE: Out of balance, Scorpios can give in to addictions, obsessions, and infatuations. Remember, obsessions are not bad in and of themselves; just make sure they are healthy ones.

Sun in Scorpio

OCTOBER 22, 2020

GO DEEPER, LEARN MORE!

The Sun is the heart center of the chart. When it is in the Sign of Scorpio, it activates my

_____ House, which governs _____

_____. When

this House is activated by the Sun, this area of experience will be illuminated. One sentence

to describe how I can make the most of this energy is _____

_____

_____.

Read more about the energies of the Sun, Scorpio, and this House in Heather Arielle's Guidebook for The Fundamentals of Astrology.

29 Thursday | October

30 Friday

31 Saturday

Full Moon in Taurus 10:49 AM

VENUS IN LIBRA (OCT 27)

Venus rules love, relationships, money, and art. When it is in the Zodiac Sign of Libra, the Sign it rules, it's time to bring equality and balance to your partnerships. Venus in Libra favors collaborations of all kinds.

GO DEEPER, LEARN MORE!

When Venus is in the Sign of Libra, it activates my _____

House, which governs _____

_____

One sentence to describe this aspect for me personally is _____

_____

_____

November

1 Sunday

Weekly Inspiration: "Inspire and prepare me for the week."

2 Monday

3 Tuesday

Mercury Direct in Libra 12:49 PM

4 Wednesday

5 Thursday

6 Friday

7 Saturday

8 Sunday | November

Weekly Inspiration: "Inspire and prepare me for the week."

9 Monday

10 Tuesday   *Mercury enters Scorpio 4:55 PM (see page 127)*

11 Wednesday

12 Thursday

13 Friday   *Mars Direct in Aries 7:35 PM*

14 Saturday

MERCURY IN SCORPIO (NOV 10)

Mercury rules communication, short-distance travel, siblings, and youth. When it is in the intense Zodiac Sign of Scorpio, communication can become secretive and thoughts can become obsessive. Need to know more about a subject? Mercury in Scorpio is an ideal time to dig deep and do the research. Hidden truths can be revealed now.

GO DEEPER, LEARN MORE!

When Mercury is in the Sign of Scorpio, it activates my _____ House, which governs

_____.

One sentence to describe this aspect for me personally is _____

_____

_____.

Read more about these energies in Heather Arielle's Guidebook for The Fundamentals of Astrology.

15 Sunday | November   *New Moon in Scorpio 12:07 AM (see page 129)*

Weekly Inspiration: "Inspire and prepare me for the week."

16 Monday

17 Tuesday

18 Wednesday

19 Thursday

20 Friday

21 Saturday   *Venus enters Scorpio 8:22 AM (see page 131)*
                                        Sun enters Sagittarius 3:40 PM (see pages 132 & 133)

New Moon Oracle Spread

The two weeks between a New and Full moon is a wonderful time to begin new things. Whatever you start will grow and blossom! Perform the New Moon Oracle Spread each month to learn which energies will be most beneficial to bring into your life during a particular New Moon phase.

Instructions

Separate the cards into categories indicated by the border color, and place in piles.

- The 4 Element cards have melon borders.
- The 3 Modality cards have dark green borders.
- The 11 Planet cards have light blue borders.
- The 12 Zodiac Sign cards have purple borders.
- The 12 House cards have light green borders.

You will not need the other cards for this spread.

CREATE YOUR SPREAD

Card 1:   Place the Reversed Moon card.
Card 2:   Select one Element card.
Card 3:   Select one Modality card.
Card 4:   Select one Planet card.
Card 5:   Select one Zodiac Sign card.
Card 6:   Select one House Card.

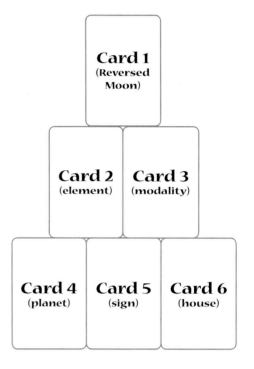

Record and Interpret Your Spread

Card 1: The Moon is the most intricate celestial body to master and is mythically connected to the Roman goddess Diana/Greek goddess Artemis. Its receptive qualities often mask its true meaning. The Reversed Card Message, "I Can See Clearly Now" is especially appropriate for New Moon energy. After all, "The fog is lifting. You'll soon have the answers you need to make an informed decision."

Card 2: The Element to incorporate during this New Moon phase is _____.

Two qualities of this Element that I'm being encouraged to embrace are _____

_____.

Card 3: The Modality to incorporate is _____.

Two qualities of this Modality that I'm being inspired to embrace are _____

_____.

Card 4: The Planet's energies to incorporate is_____.

Two qualities of this Planet that I can embrace are _____

_____.

Card 5: The Zodiac Sign that will be of most benefit to me right now is _____.

Three qualities represented by this Sign are _____

_____.

Is there **someone close to me** that resonates to the energy of this Sign? If so, who? _____

_____.

Card 6: The House that will be of most benefit is the _____ House. The area of experi-

ence represented by this House is _____

_____

Some activities I can do or actions I can take to activate the energy in this House are _____

_____.

Putting It All Together
Is there a theme? What do you think is the overall message of this New Moon spread?

VENUS IN SCORPIO (NOV 21)

Venus rules love, relationships, money, and art. When it is in the Sign of Scorpio, it's time to allow transformation into your relationships. You are being encouraged to love intensely and passionately.

GO DEEPER, LEARN MORE!

When Venus is in the Sign of Scorpio, it activates my _____ House, which governs

_____.

One sentence to describe this aspect for me personally is _____

_____.

Read more about the energies of Venus, Scorpio, and this House in Heather Arielle's Guidebook for The Fundamentals of Astrology.

Sagittarius
Time To Explore

Embrace your inner wanderer.
Like a wild horse, you are meant to roam free.

Get Intimate!
Open your heart to partnership, collaboration,
and, yes, gulp, true intimacy.

Sagittarius

On November 21, the Sun moves into Sagittarius, the ninth Sign of the Zodiac, and remains there until December 21. The intense and transformative energy of Scorpio is transmuted into the expansive and effervescent energy of Sagittarius.

Planet: Jupiter
House: Ninth
Element: Fire
Modality: Mutable

Jupiter

IN BALANCE: In balance, Sagittarians are full of energy, optimism, honesty, and the endless desire to spread their wings. They develop high ideals and pursue them with the use of their immense, fiery energy.

OUT OF BALANCE: Out of balance, Sagittarians can take the desire for freedom to such an extreme that even the idea of partnership can seem like a ball and chain scenario.

Sun in Sagittarius

NOVEMBER 21, 2020

Sun
Shine Your Light Brightly
Celebrate this time of good health, blessings, and much deserved success.

Masculine Energy
A male relative or friend may be in need of your support or guidance.

Sagittarius
Time To Explore
Embrace your inner wanderer.
Like a wild horse, you are meant to roam free.

Get Intimate!
Open your heart to partnership, collaboration, and, yes, gulp, true intimacy.

House Card

GO DEEPER, LEARN MORE!

The Sun is the heart center of the chart. When it is in the Sign of Sagittarius, it activates my

_____ House, which governs _____

_____. When

this House is activated by the Sun, this area of experience will be illuminated. One sentence

to describe how I can make the most of this energy is _____

_____

_____.

Read more about the energies of the Sun, Sagittarius, and this House in Heather Arielle's Guidebook for The Fundamentals of Astrology.

22 Sunday | November

Weekly Inspiration: "Inspire and prepare me for the week."

23 Monday

24 Tuesday

25 Wednesday

26 Thursday

27 Friday

28 Saturday

29 Sunday | November

Weekly Inspiration: "Inspire and prepare me for the week."

30 Monday   *Full Moon Penumbral Lunar Eclipse in Gemini 4:30 AM*

Have you ordered your 2021 Astrology Oracle Card Planner?
Available in print or as a digital download from AriellesAstrology.com.

MERCURY IN SAGITTARIUS (DEC 1)

Mercury rules communication, short-distance travel, siblings, and youth. When it is in the expansive Sign of Sagittarius, higher learning and philosophical thinking are favored. It's also easier to see the big picture; so, make sure when communicating your plans, you don't miss any details.

GO DEEPER, LEARN MORE!

When Mercury is in the Sign of Sagittarius, it activates my _____ House, which governs

_____.

One sentence to describe this aspect for me personally is _____

_____.

Read more about these energies in Heather Arielle's Guidebook for The Fundamentals of Astrology.

December

1 Tuesday   *Mercury enters Sagittarius 2:51 PM (see page 136)*

2 Wednesday

3 Thursday

4 Friday

5 Saturday

6 Sunday

Weekly Inspiration: "Inspire and prepare me for the week."

7 Monday

8 Tuesday | December

9 Wednesday

10 Thursday

11 Friday

12 Saturday

13 Sunday

Weekly Inspiration: "Inspire and prepare me for the week."

14 Monday

New Moon Total Solar Eclipse in Sagittarius 11:16 AM (see page 139)

New Moon Oracle Spread

The two weeks between a New and Full moon is a wonderful time to begin new things. Whatever you start will grow and blossom! Perform the New Moon Oracle Spread each month to learn which energies will be most beneficial to bring into your life during a particular New Moon phase.

Instructions

Separate the cards into categories indicated by the border color, and place in piles.

- The 4 Element cards have melon borders.
- The 3 Modality cards have dark green borders.
- The 11 Planet cards have light blue borders.
- The 12 Zodiac Sign cards have purple borders.
- The 12 House cards have light green borders.

You will not need the other cards for this spread.

CREATE YOUR SPREAD

Card 1:   Place the Reversed Moon card.
Card 2:   Select one Element card.
Card 3:   Select one Modality card.
Card 4:   Select one Planet card.
Card 5:   Select one Zodiac Sign card.
Card 6:   Select one House Card.

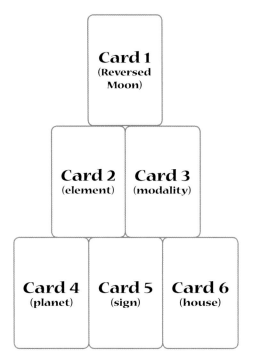

Record and Interpret Your Spread

Card 1: The Moon is the most intricate celestial body to master and is mythically connected to the Roman goddess Diana/Greek goddess Artemis. Its receptive qualities often mask its true meaning. The Reversed Card Message, "I Can See Clearly Now" is especially appropriate for New Moon energy. After all, "The fog is lifting. You'll soon have the answers you need to make an informed decision."

Card 2: The Element to incorporate during this New Moon phase is _____.

Two qualities of this Element that I'm being encouraged to embrace are _____

_____.

Card 3: The Modality to incorporate is _____.

Two qualities of this Modality that I'm being inspired to embrace are _____

_____.

Card 4: The Planet's energies to incorporate is_____.

Two qualities of this Planet that I can embrace are _____

_____.

Card 5: The Zodiac Sign that will be of most benefit to me right now is _____.

Three qualities represented by this Sign are _____

_____.

Is there **someone close to me** that resonates to the energy of this Sign? If so, who? _____

_____.

Card 6: The House that will be of most benefit is the _____ House. The area of experience represented by this House is _____

_____

Some activities I can do or actions I can take to activate the energy in this House are _____

_____.

Putting It All Together
Is there a theme? What do you think is the overall message of this New Moon spread?

15 Tuesday | December   *Venus enters Sagittarius 11:21 AM (see page 142)*

16 Wednesday

17 Thursday

18 Friday

19 Saturday

20 Sunday   *Mercury enters Capricorn 6:07 PM (see page 142)*

Weekly Inspiration: "Inspire and prepare me for the week."

21 Monday   *Sun enters Capricorn 5:02 AM (see pages 143 & 144)*

VENUS IN SAGITTARIUS (DEC 15)

Venus rules love, relationships, money, and art. When it is in the Zodiac Sign of Sagittarius, it's time to explore. Find fun and creative ways to bring higher levels of freedom into your relationships. Also, develop partnerships with people who are quite different from yourself.

GO DEEPER, LEARN MORE!

When Venus is in the Sign of Sagittarius, it activates my _____

House, which governs _____

_____

One sentence to describe this aspect for me personally is _____

_____

_____

MERCURY IN CAPRICORN (DEC 20)

Mercury rules communication, short-distance travel, siblings, and youth. When it is in the practical Zodiac Sign of Capricorn, thinking can become more serious. Be inspired by the reality check.

GO DEEPER, LEARN MORE!

When Mercury is in the Sign of Capricorn, it activates my _____

House, which governs _____

_____

One sentence to describe this aspect for me personally is _____

_____

_____

Read more about the energies of these Planets, Signs, and Houses in Heather Arielle's Guidebook for The Fundamentals of Astrology.

Capricorn
Climb Every Mountain

It's time to be the mountain goat and begin your ascent.

Your ego is strong enough to survive a healthy dose of constructive criticism.

Humble Pie

Capricorn

Saturn

On December 21, the Sun moves into Capricorn, the tenth Sign of the Zodiac, and remains there until January 19. The expansive and optimistic energy of Sagittarius is transformed into the sober, practical, and restrictive energy of Capricorn. Ruled by Saturn, Capricorn is an earthy, sensible Sign, imparting its natives with all the tools they need to manifest in the real world.

Planet: Saturn
House: Tenth
Element: Earth
Modality: Cardinal

IN BALANCE: In balance, Capricorns are wonderful self-starters. They are revered as the sages and elders of their community.

OUT OF BALANCE: Out of balance, they can begin to view their Capricorn talent for methodical self-discipline as more of a burden than a gift.

Sun in Capricorn

DECEMBER 21, 2020

GO DEEPER, LEARN MORE!

The Sun is the heart center of the chart. When it is in the Sign of Capricorn, it activates my

_____ House, which governs _____

_____. When

this House is activated by the Sun, this area of experience will be illuminated. One sentence

to describe how I can make the most of this energy is _____

_____

_____.

Read more about the energies of the Sun, Capricorn, and this House in Heather Arielle's Guidebook for The Fundamentals of Astrology.

22 Tuesday | December

23 Wednesday

24 Thursday

25 Friday

26 Saturday

27 Sunday

Weekly Inspiration: "Inspire and prepare me for the week."

28 Monday

Full Moon in Cancer 10:28 PM

30 Wednesday

31 Thursday

The 12-Month Astrology Spread

This is a great spread to do if you'd like to get a preview of your year ahead.

Create Your Spread

Beginning with Card 1 in the first month position, draw one card for each month, creating a circle. Place a final card in the Center of the circle. The Center card will give you an overall theme for your year. If you'd like further clarification, you can draw second and third cards for each month. If you do this, remember to add second and third cards in the Center, as well.

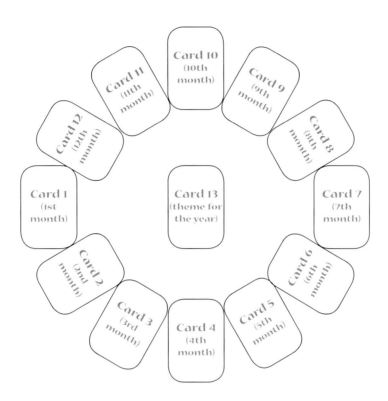

Record and Interpret Your Spread

Fill in the card for each month and the theme of the year.

1. January _____

2. February _____

3. March _____

4. April _____

5. May _____

6. June _____

7. July _____

8. August _____

9. September _____

10. October _____

11. November _____

12. December _____

13. Theme of the Year _____

For each card, describe its inspirational meaning in one sentence.

1. _____

2. _____

3. _____

4. _____

5. _____

6. _____

7. _____

8. _____

9. _____

10. _____

11. _____

12. _____

13. _____

Putting It All Together
What is the overall message of this spread for you?

January 2021

1 Friday

2 Saturday

3 Sunday

Weekly Inspiration: "Inspire and prepare me for the week."

4 Monday

5 Tuesday

6 Wednesday

Mars enters Taurus 5:27 PM (see page 150)

7 Thursday

Mars
Get Physical!

Walk, run, swim, or try your hand in the ring.
It's time to get moving.

Assert Yourself

A conflict is brewing. Time to face it head-on.
The situation will be resolved in your favor.

Taurus
Cornucopia of Riches

Be tenacious. You have the stamina to
manifest your dreams.

No Bullies Allowed!

You or someone close to you may be
trying to control the situation.

MARS IN TAURUS (JAN 6, 2021)

Mars is the planet of action, sexuality, sports, and war. When it is in the Zodiac Sign of Taurus, it is in its detriment, making it harder for the planet to express its forward momentum. So instead, when Mars is in this steadfast Sign, slow down, focus, and pursue your goals with perseverance and tenacity.

GO DEEPER, LEARN MORE!

When Mars is in the Sign of Taurus, it activates my _____ House, which governs

_____.

One sentence to describe this aspect for me personally is _____

_____.

Read more about these energies in Heather Arielle's Guidebook for The Fundamentals of Astrology.

8 Friday | January

Mercury enters Aquarius 7:00 AM (see page 152)
Venus enters Capricorn 10:41 AM (see page 152)

9 Saturday

10 Sunday

Weekly Inspiration: "Inspire and prepare me for the week."

11 Monday

12 Tuesday

13 Wednesday

New Moon in Capricorn (see page 153)

14 Thursday

MERCURY IN AQUARIUS (JAN 8)

Mercury rules communication, short-distance travel, siblings, and youth. When it is in the unique and humanitarian Zodiac Sign of Aquarius, independent thinking is supported. Embrace intellectual pursuits and share your most unconventional and alternative ideas.

GO DEEPER, LEARN MORE!

When Mercury is in the Sign of Aquarius, it activates my _____

House, which governs _____

_____

One sentence to describe this aspect for me personally is _____

_____

_____

VENUS IN CAPRICORN (JAN 8)

Venus rules love, relationships, money, and art. When it is in the Zodiac Sign of Capricorn, it's time to get serious about both love and money. Conservative investments are favored, especially ones that pay out over a long time, such as an annuity. Concerning love, embrace your inner adult and work to make partnerships in your life long-lasting.

GO DEEPER, LEARN MORE!

When Venus is in the Sign of Capricorn, it activates my _____

House, which governs _____

_____

One sentence to describe this aspect for me personally is _____

_____

_____

Read more about these energies in Heather Arielle's Guidebook for The Fundamentals of Astrology.

New Moon Oracle Spread

The two weeks between a New and Full moon is a wonderful time to begin new things. Whatever you start will grow and blossom! Perform the New Moon Oracle Spread each month to learn which energies will be most beneficial to bring into your life during a particular New Moon phase.

Instructions

Separate the cards into categories indicated by the border color, and place in piles.

- The 4 Element cards have melon borders.
- The 3 Modality cards have dark green borders.
- The 11 Planet cards have light blue borders.
- The 12 Zodiac Sign cards have purple borders.
- The 12 House cards have light green borders.

You will not need the other cards for this spread.

CREATE YOUR SPREAD

Card 1: Place the Reversed Moon card.
Card 2: Select one Element card.
Card 3: Select one Modality card.
Card 4: Select one Planet card.
Card 5: Select one Zodiac Sign card.
Card 6: Select one House Card.

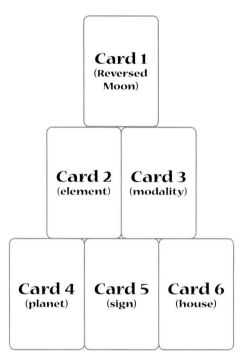

Record and Interpret Your Spread

Card 1: The Moon is the most intricate celestial body to master and is mythically connected to the Roman goddess Diana/Greek goddess Artemis. Its receptive qualities often mask its true meaning. The Reversed Card Message, "I Can See Clearly Now" is especially appropriate for New Moon energy. After all, "The fog is lifting. You'll soon have the answers you need to make an informed decision."

Card 2: The Element to incorporate during this New Moon phase is _____.

Two qualities of this Element that I'm being encouraged to embrace are _____

_____.

Card 3: The Modality to incorporate is _____.

Two qualities of this Modality that I'm being inspired to embrace are _____

_____.

Card 4: The Planet's energies to incorporate is_____.

Two qualities of this Planet that I can embrace are _____

_____.

Card 5: The Zodiac Sign that will be of most benefit to me right now is _____.

Three qualities represented by this Sign are _____

_____.

Is there **someone close to me** that resonates to the energy of this Sign? If so, who? _____

_____.

Card 6: The House that will be of most benefit is the _____ House. The area of experi-

ence represented by this House is _____

_____

Some activities I can do or actions I can take to activate the energy in this House are _____

_____.

Putting It All Together
Is there a theme? What do you think is the overall message of this New Moon spread?

16 Friday | January
_____

16 Saturday
_____

17 Sunday
_____
Weekly Inspiration: "Inspire and prepare me for the week."

18 Monday
_____

19 Tuesday   *Sun enters Aquarius 3:40 PM (see page 156 & 157)*
_____

20 Wednesday
_____

21 Thursday
_____

Aquarius
To Thine Own Self Be True

No one sees the world quite the way you do.
Celebrate your unique voice & one-of-a-kind style.

Rebel With a Cause

Channel your desire to go against the grain.
Join a humanitarian group or start one yourself.

Aquarius

On January 19, 2021, the Sun moves into Aquarius, the eleventh Sign of the Zodiac, and remains there until February 18. The traditional and adult energy of Capricorn is transformed into the unconventional and rebellious energy of Aquarius.

Planet: Uranus, co-ruler Saturn
House: Eleventh
Element: Air
Modality: Fixed

Uranus

IN BALANCE: In balance, Aquarians are champions of the underdog and relentlessly pursue humanitarian causes. In other words, an in-balance Aquarian is a rebel with a cause.

OUT OF BALANCE: Out of balance, Aquarians are still rebellious; only, alas, they tend to lose sight of their cause.

Sun in Aquarius

JANUARY 19, 2021

GO DEEPER, LEARN MORE!

The Sun is the heart center of the chart. When it is in the Sign of Aquarius, it activates my

_____ House, which governs _____

_____. When

this House is activated by the Sun, this area of experience will be illuminated. One sentence

to describe how I can make the most of this energy is _____

_____

_____.

Read more about these energies in Heather Arielle's Guidebook for The Fundamentals of Astrology.

22 Friday | January
_____

23 Saturday
_____

24 Sunday
_____
Weekly Inspiration: "Inspire and prepare me for the week."

25 Monday
_____

26 Tuesday
_____

27 Wednesday
_____

28 Thursday
_____ *Full Moon in Leo 2:16 PM*

29 Friday | January

30 Saturday   *Mercury goes Retrograde 10:52 AM (see page 160)*

31 Sunday

Weekly Inspiration: "Inspire and prepare me for the week."

Mercury Retrograde Oracle Spread

Reimagine, Reignite, Rejuvenate

Mercury goes retrograde in Aquarius from January 30, 2021 to February 21. Perform this spread to help you focus on the areas ruled by Mercury (writing, thinking, learning, and communicating of all kinds) that are in most need of reflection and review.

*The most important thing to remember about ALL retrogrades is how the word begins—*RE*. And every word that begins with these magical two letters is not just your friend, but your best friend. If you can *RE* it—you can do it!

CREATE YOUR SPREAD

- Place the Upright Mercury Retrograde card in what will be the Center card position.
- Shuffle the remaining cards.
- Creating a 5-pointed star, place the cards in a circle around the Center card, starting with the top-right position.

Card 1:   Area of reflection.
Card 2:   Area of reconnection.
Card 3:   Area to reignite.
Card 4:   Area of refinement.
Card 5:   Path to rejuvenation.

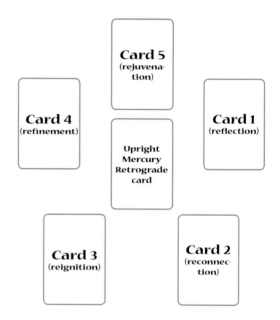

Record and Interpret Your Spread

Once you've completed the spread, fill in the card for each area.

1. Focus of reflection: _____

2. Area of reconnection: _____

3. Area to reignite: _____

4. Area to refine: _____

5. Path to rejuvenation: _____

For each card, describe its inspirational meaning in one sentence.

1. _____

2. _____

3. _____

4. _____

5. _____

Putting It All Together

Is there a theme? What do you think is the overall message of this Mercury Retrograde spread?

Share your spreads and readings with us on Social Media!
Use **#houseofastrology** so we can share with our online community.

Stay in Touch

Learn more about Arielle's Astrology, and schedule a reading
with Heather Arielle at AriellesAstrology.com.

Visit HouseOfAstrology.com
• Get a free online Card of the Day inspirational reading
• Order full-color posters of the artwork from
The Fundamentals of Astrology Oracle Deck
• Join our mailing list to learn about
upcoming Oracle Deck releases

Follow Heather Arielle on Facebook at
Facebook.com/AriellesAstrology.

The Fundamentals of Astrology Oracle Deck is available
online from Amazon.com, or you can reach
the publisher at LuminousMoon.com.

About the Author

Heather Arielle is the founder and CEO of Arielle's Astrology. She offers Astrology Readings, Astrology Counseling, and Astrology Classes and Workshops. Her readings focus on personal, practical, and powerful ways astrology can improve your daily life.

Television Appearances:
- Open Minds with Regina Meredith
- Beyond Belief with George Noory

Radio Interviews:
- Coast to Coast AM with George Noory
- Healing From Within with Tony Valen
- Conscious Evolution Radio with Ann Gelsheimer

Presentations:
- "Tools for Achieving Higher Consciousness" at StarworksUSA UFO Symposium in Laughlin, Nevada (2017)
- "Contact and Consciousness: Transformation Through Astrology" at BoulderExo in Boulder, Colorado (2015)
- "Consciousness and the Stars: The Energy of Transformation" at StarworksUSA UFO Symposium in Laughlin, Nevada (2014)

Heather Arielle is also a Drama Desk-nominated and published playwright. Her plays have been performed at numerous theaters across the country, as well as abroad.

In addition to her playwriting, astrological readings, and presentations, Heather Arielle teaches songwriting for Lincoln Center Theater and is a member of the BMI Musical Theater Workshop. She received her M.F.A. from Columbia University, where she was a Presidential Scholar. As an undergraduate at the University of Michigan, she was the recipient of two Hopwood Drama Awards.

About the Collaboration

Q: What do you get when you cross a Gemini with an Aquarius?
A: A unique, playful, and whimsical Oracle Deck.

Thom Cummins and I have known each other for quite some time, and our relationship has always been a dynamic and supportive one.

In astrological terms, our Suns (Aquarius and Gemini) form a 120 degree aspect known as a trine. When trines form between two people, a gift is theirs for the taking. But as I like to say, "Just don't forget to open it." Well, guess what, I forgot to do just that! I forgot to follow through with one of my most basic tenets.

So although Thom and I share a rich and meaningful history, we never truly manifested the trine—the gift between us—until now with this magical collaboration.

Trines are harmonious aspects because they connect energies that are in the same element. Aquarius and Gemini are both Air signs. As Air signs, Thom and I are verbal, social, and intellectually curious. We delight in exploring and developing ideas through endless discussion and debate.

Our Moon signs oppose one another, Thom's in Sagittarius and mine in Gemini (like my Sun). Gemini and Sagittarius are playful, whimsical signs and complete one another in the traditional yin and yang way.

Both of these signs honor freedom, and that's one thing we gave generously to each other. I never interfered or dictated what Thom would paint; and in return, he gave me free reign to put into words my responses to his paintings. By allowing each of us the freedom to contribute our individual talents, we were able to create an inspired work that represents a true blend of our talents and energies.

I thank Thom for manifesting the trine and opening this beautiful gift with me. I hope you enjoy our unique, innovative, and dynamic creation. In the words of the artist Thom Cummins, "Have fun and dance every day." We certainly did while creating this!

When Gemini and Capricorn Team Up: The Magic of the Inconjunct

My publisher, Carolyn Oakley (Luminous Moon Press) has her Sun in Capricorn, while my Sun is in Gemini. The key to our successful and creative partnership? Blending what may at first appear to be unblendable energy. Serious, practical, and wise Capricorns can find the playful, childlike, and mercurial energy of Geminis a bit too frivolous for their tastes. Geminis can see Capricorns as controlling, often wondering why they can't just lighten up a bit and go more with the flow. As my publisher, Carolyn has helped me to manifest my Gemini ideas in practical ways that have resulted in our creating a tangible product, my oracle deck, The Fundamentals of Astrology. So, the next time you partner with someone whose Sun makes an Inconjunct (150 degree aspect) with your Sun, follow this simple rule: don't choose one side or the other; find a way to blend the two energies, and you will embrace the magic of this special astrological aspect.

I Am Here As a Resource!

Want to learn more? I invite you to schedule a full-length reading, sign up for a private astrology class, or participate in one of my workshops that are offered online and in-person. Call 917-546-6797 or book online at AriellesAstrology.com.

Visit my websites, AriellesAstrology.com and HouseOfAstrology.com to learn more about my approach, watch videos, read articles, and to experience much more.

I am also available on Facebook, YouTube, Instagram, and Pinterest. Use **#houseofastrology** and we will share your oracle card spreads and readings with our online community!

- Facebook.com/AriellesAstrology
- YouTube.com/user/AriellesAstrology
- Instagram.com/HouseOfAstrology
- Pinterest.com/AstroArielle

Photo by Aleanna Collins

Made in the USA
Coppell, TX
04 November 2020